Christmas ~~in New York~~

New York 2024

A Pocket Guide for Fun Places to Visit, Must do Activities, and Hidden Gems

J. Jose Rios Wander

For both a first-time visitor and experienced visitors, this guide aims to maximize a budget-friendly Christmas vacation to New York. The city comes with an abundance of chances to make priceless memories, through famous Christmas lights, lively districts and a rich cultural legacy. A variety of reasonably priced choices, like affordable lodging, fun activities, and fascinating activities, have been carefully described. With suggestions on well-known holiday destinations as well as hidden treasures where visitors will be able to escape the crowd and give their holiday experience something special.

To help prepare visitors more easily and enjoyably, this guide also offers helpful suggestions with budgets in mind, learning when the ideal time is to visit, tips for getting affordable flights, and ways to make use of all the available city transit alternatives. You can easily tour the city using Google Maps since there are scannable QR codes for each site described. You'll be able to enjoy the wonder of New York at Christmas more and fret about the details less.

CONTENTS

PLANNING YOUR TRIP

Christmas Magic and Culture

Christmastime in New York is really beautiful; the joy of the season seems to pervade every street, building, and area of the city. Visiting New York during the holidays is a once-in-a-lifetime experience that mixes the grandeur of the city with the kindness and pleasure of Christmas. The splendor of New York during Christmas is in the huge window displays of department stores like Saks Fifth Avenue and Macy's; in the bright lights that cover the city's unique skyline; and in the sound of street corner carolers singing.

It's the way the city, which is busy and frenzied the rest of the year, seems to settle down a bit to enjoy the positive mood. The Rockefeller Center Christmas Tree is the most famous sight linked with Christmas in New York. A giant evergreen is cut, brought into the heart of the city, and decked with thousands of lights each year. At the tree-lighting event, when the switch is flipped, the entire city appears to shine with joyful happiness. Travelers from all over gather to observe the tree, skate on the ice rink underneath it, and feel something greater: a moment of joy shared by all at a well-known spot. Walking around Central Park in the winter is an especially amazing experience. A green haven in the middle of the city, the park is transformed into a winter dream filled with horse-drawn carts, frozen ponds, and walks coated in snow. The park makes for a quiet haven where you can take in the beauty of the season in a more private environment; its peace is a pleasing contrast to the busy city nearby.

The draw is enhanced by the Christmas markets that grow up all across the city, particularly the Columbus Circle and Union Square markets. These markets are packed with sellers offering a broad variety of items, especially holiday treats as well as handmade goods, and are the perfect place to buy one-of-a-kind gifts or to soak in the joyful feelings. The authentic spirit of New York during Christmas resides not only in the lights and decorations, but also in its culture. The way the city celebrates the holidays is a great representation of the range of nations that make up New York. No matter where you're from, you'll likely discover parts of your own holiday customs in New York. There's a wonderful sense of friendship throughout the holidays. Christmas is a time when people come together in a place that may seem cold. It's clear in the neighborhoods where locals go all out with the décor, making gorgeous displays that lure tourists from all across the city. This is particularly well-known in Brooklyn's Dyker Heights, where houses are fully decked out with lights, inflatables, and Christmas ornaments.

The people love sharing the season's happiness with others and take great pleasure in their performances. New York's artistic groups are also a key component of the Christmas events. For years, audiences have been enthralled by the valuable custom of the Radio City Christmas Spectacular that features the well-regarded Rockettes. The concert is a magnificent showcase of precision dancing, festive music, and a positive mood, all set in one of the most famous places in New York. The "Nutcracker," performed by the New York City Ballet, is another artistic wonder. Numerous families make sure to watch this famous dance during the holidays due to its hypnotic music and excellent routines. Generations of New Yorkers and tourists have enjoyed the moment of pure Christmas pleasure that is Clara's journey through the Land of Sweets, backed by the charmed Tchaikovsky symphony. But the New York Christmas culture setting is marked by more than only the large-scale shows. It's also smaller, more personal experiences, like quiet times of thought in one of the city's endless old churches, jazz bands playing Christmas music in warm bars, or unplanned performances at train stops. These meetings give meaning to the Christmas season, giving a time for community, prayer, and company in addition to joy.

The way the city handles visitors of varied backgrounds and faiths is one of the most amazing things about New York during Christmas. The most obvious holiday is Christmas, although the city also marks Hanukkah, Kwanzaa, and Diwali. Menorahs could be seen in public places, Kwanzaa parties are held at cultural groups, and happy events that show the city's vast diversity are all present. Part of what makes New York unique is its inclusiveness;

regardless of race or holiday, everyone can feel at home here. This range is repeated in New York's food culture as well. Throughout the holidays, you can eat traditional Christmas meals as well as try new tastes, and the city's food scene is a feast for the senses.

Budgeting for Your Christmas Adventure

It's no secret that the city can grow expensive, especially during Christmas. But, with a little planning and careful money management, you can experience the energy of a New York Christmas without breaking the bank. The sooner you start planning, the better when it comes to spending for a Christmas trip to New York. The city is a famous Christmas resort, and as December comes nearer, rates for travel, lodgings, and activities normally climb substantially. By arranging your holiday many months in advance, you'll be able to acquire lower deals and keep clear of last-minute price spikes that might drastically strain your funds.

Look for flight deals, and try utilizing cost comparison programs like Google Flights or Skyscanner. Flying into other airports other than JFK, such as LaGuardia (LGA) or Newark (EWR), can also save you money. Try to book trips during the week if your calendar is open, as they are usually less costly than outings on the weekends. Buying an endless MetroCard is a reasonable option. For roughly $33, a 7-day unlimited ticket gives unrestricted access to the metro and buses, and that will be excellent for a week-long stay. This way, you won't have to worry about rising transportation costs while seeing the city.

The fact that so many of New York's most wonderful Christmastime events are either free or relatively cheap is one of its best traits.

- The Rockefeller Center Christmas Tree is a well-known New York holiday draw, and entry is free. Admire this big, beautifully decorated tree. If you're lucky, you might be able to attend a nearby live show or holiday party.

- The Fifth Avenue Christmas window decorations are a beautiful sight. Retailers like Bergdorf Goodman, Saks Fifth Avenue, and Macy's change their shops into beautiful Christmas sets that are really works of art. Walking along Fifth Avenue and taking in these lights is free; it's a wonderful way to get into the Christmas spirit.

- Not only are the Christmas markets in New York excellent places to find one-of-a-kind things, but you can visit them for free. Some of the best are the Holiday Shops at Bryant Park, the Union Square Holiday Market, and the Columbus Circle Holiday Market. You can explore these markets, take in the joyful atmosphere, and possibly even score a few reasonably priced memories.

During the holiday, many stores in New York offer significant deals, especially around Black Friday and after Christmas. If you're in the city around these times, take advantage of the deals to save on gifts or souvenirs.

Best Times to Visit During the Holidays

Christmastime in New York is like a winter dream: there's a lovely mood, the city twinkles with lights, and there seems to be holiday excitement everywhere you turn. And with all of that, choosing when to visit is a problem that comes along with all this excitement:

❖ **Thanksgiving Weekend:**

Thanksgiving Weekend is the best time to visit before the holidays fully begin. Commencing in 1924, the Macy's Thanksgiving Day Parade has been a lovely way to start off the holiday in New York. Manhattan's streets are filled with giant balloons, bright floats, and marching bands, making for a pretty amazing sight. Thanksgiving weekend usually runs from the fourth Thursday in November until the following Sunday. So, Thanksgiving weekend will be from Thursday, November 28th, through Sunday, December 1st. During this weekend, the city comes alive with a Christmas mood. The city's Christmas trees light up, and many shops show their colorful window displays directly after Thanksgiving. With Black

Friday deals, it's also a fantastic time to start your Christmas shopping early. Remember that Thanksgiving weekend is one of the biggest weekends in New York, so be prepared for bigger groups and more costly accommodation. If you want to watch the show, arrive early to ensure a good location along the road.

- ❖ **Early December:**

Early December is the best time to take advantage of the holiday parties without the crush of tourists during the popular time of year. The first two weeks of December contain all the wonderful pleasure of the holidays, with a bit less crowd. The holiday markets are packed, the ice rinks are open, and the Rockefeller Center Christmas Tree is lit. For individuals who prefer to fully accept the Christmas spirit while still having some breathing room, early December is excellent. All the usual Christmas activities, like watching Bryant Park's Winter Village or visiting "The Nutcracker," will be available to you without feeling overwhelmed by crowds. Early December is still a popular time to visit, even if it's less busy than later in the month, so it's a smart idea to organize your hotel and any must-do activities in advance.

❖ **Mid-December to Christmas:**

The peak of the holiday season is from mid-December to Christmas. The happy mood is at its best, and the city is fully dressed out in lights. If you want to be right in the middle of everything and experience the city at its liveliest, now is the best time to visit. The days going up to Christmas in New York are rather great.nThere's a clear excitement in the air, the Christmas window decorations are at their best, and carolers fill the streets with music, and you'll believe you're in a Christmas movie. Keep in mind that this is the busiest and most expensive time of year to visit New York. Attractions will get busy, and accommodations might fill up quickly. You should prepare early and expect long lines at major places if you wish to visit during this time.

❖ **Christmas Week:**

Christmas week is an excellent time to visit. It would be a once-in-a-lifetime event to wake up on

Christmas morning to the sight of sparkling lights and snow-covered streets. New York during Christmas week is absolutely wonderful. As people enjoy the holiday, the city slows down a bit, allowing you to witness a more calm side. One of the city's famous churches is having a Christmas Eve service, Central Park changed into a winter picture, and the holiday markets will be at their busiest. The days immediately before and just after Christmas are among the most expensive for travel, so plan your Christmas meals and activities ahead of time, as a lot of businesses and places close on Christmas Day.

❖ **New Years Eve:**

New Year's Eve in New York is an occasion unlike any other for those eager to finish out the year on a high note. The Times Square ball drop is a must-do event, bringing visitors from all over to the never-sleeping city to ring in the New Year. New York is electric on New Year's Eve. There are activities everywhere in this lively city, and you'll be part of one of the world's best events. Note that Times Square in particular gets pretty crowded on New Year's Eve. Be ready for hours of cold waiting if you want to be in Times Square for the ball drop (and keep in mind that there aren't many bathrooms there). For a more relaxed party, think about going on a New Year's Eve boat or to a rooftop bar.

❖ **After New Year's:**

To take in the bright décor without the throng, it's a good idea to visit shortly after New Year's. Take advantage of the chance to enjoy the Christmas mood in a more laid-back setting, since some sites and landmarks in the city stay open until early January. There's less noise and more calm during the first week of January. You can still enjoy the Rockefeller Center Christmas Tree and other holiday lights, plus the crowds have decreased and room rates have dropped. Take advantage of post-holiday savings and explore the city at your leisure during this beautiful time of year. And while the city is quieter, the temperature can drop greatly, so dress warmly and be ready for winter.

Budget Traveler's Guide to Transportation

The train is New York City's most affordable transportation hub. For $2.90, you can go almost anywhere in the city. The rail system may seem intimidating, especially with the Christmas crowds, but it is worth it, and you'll see why once you get used to it.

- This reasonably priced transit option is often the city's quickest. During the holidays, when the streets may be congested with automobiles, the train whisks you under the chaos. Taking the train is a quintessential New York experience, contributing much to the city's allure and tempo.

- If you plan to use the system often, pick up a MetroCard at any metro station, load it with ride credit, or purchase an infinite pass. Use a rail map application, such as Citymapper or Google Maps, to arrange your route. Keep in mind that metro stations can become crowded, particularly if they're near famous places, so allow extra time to get there.

One of the best things to do in New York during the holiday is to stroll around the city's streets. The city is aglow in festive grandeur, with store displays, Christmas trees wherever you turn, and brilliant lights. Walking not only saves you money but also gives you a close-up view of the city.

- Walking is the best way to take in some of New York's most well-known holiday attractions, like the Fifth Avenue window displays, the Bryant Park ice rink, and the Rockefeller Center Christmas Tree. By strolling, you can observe all the little details that contribute to the season's distinctiveness.

- December will be chilly, so dress in layers, bring comfortable shoes, and a thermos of hot chocolate to keep warm. Plus, be aware of your surroundings and the flow of foot traffic, particularly in crowded areas like Times Square or near significant landmarks.

The New York City bus is an additional reasonably priced mode of transportation that gives a perspective of the city from a different angle. The trip's cost is the same as the train, and you can pay using a mobile payment method or your MetroCard.

- Buses are a fantastic method to see the city while moving from one place to another. This is especially true around the holidays, when the streets are gorgeously decorated. The M5 and M7 buses are great options for a lovely excursion because they go along Broadway and give stunning views of Christmas lights and decorations.

- Buses can be slower than subways during peak hours of the Christmas shopping season due to heavy traffic. When at all feasible, schedule your excursions outside of peak hour to save time. And, remember to signal the driver when you want to get off and pay attention to bus stops.

You can travel alone, with friends, or maybe because you don't want to use public transportation. Ride-sharing services like Uber and Lyft, or traditional yellow taxis, are reasonable options. They're more expensive than the bus or metro, but worth it for late-night or big-bag travel.

- Mostly after a tiring day of sightseeing, there are moments when you just want the convenience of being dropped off at your hotel door. Thus, ride-sharing services and taxis come in handy in situations where taking the bus or waiting for one isn't ideal.

- The increase in demand for ride-sharing over the Christmas season may be the cause of the price increase. To save money, try scheduling rides at off-peak times or using public transit for shorter distances. Keep in mind that tipping is customarily 15-20% of the entire fare and is anticipated if you hire a taxi.

If you're itching for a quick journey and the weather is ideal, use New York's bike-sharing program, Citi Bike. It's an enjoyable way to move around for short journeys, and it gives you a new perspective on the city.

- Riding a bike through Central Park or along the Hudson River Greenway will be an incredibly picturesque experience, more so during the winter when the park is blanketed in snow and the river is glistening with Christmas lights. Manhattan has an abundance of bike routes, making it easier than ever to get around the city safely.

- A day ticket allows you to take as many 30-minute journeys as you'd want, making them perfect for sightseeing. Make sure you dock your bike within 30 minutes to avoid additional penalties. Naturally, dress warmly and consider riding a bike in December since it will be chilly.

Take a boat ride to get a new perspective on the city. For instance, the free Staten Island Ferry provides breathtaking views of New York Harbor, the Manhattan skyline, and the Statue of Liberty.

It's a fantastic opportunity to avoid the traffic and see the city's most well-known sights.

- The boat offers a serene escape from the hustle and bustle, with a unique perspective of New York's Christmas lights and decorations from the water. Furthermore, most boat journeys are reasonably priced, and the Staten Island ferry is completely free.

- Boats might operate less often in the winter, so be careful to check timetables ahead of time and make appropriate arrangements. Try to ride the Staten Island Ferry around sunset for the finest views of the Statue of Liberty and the city.

Whatever your chosen method of transportation, remember that the journey itself makes up half the fun of visiting New York over the holidays. By combining several modes of transportation, you can save money while still enjoying the city's seasonal splendor.

What to Pack for a Winter Wonderland

Planning a winter vacation to New York is like stepping into a nativity scene; complete with bright lights, happy music, and the alluring aroma of freshly cooked chestnuts being sold by street vendors. Making sure you have everything you need to survive New York's often wonderful and difficult winter is crucial to be warm, comfortable, and prepared for adventures.

- The chilly weather is erratic. A clear, sunny day is probable, but you might also experience freezing temperatures, brisk winds, or perhaps light showers. The secret to being warm and cozy is layering, it also lets you wear different outfits depending on the weather.

- Start with fully-covered, snug-fitting trousers and warm shirts. To keep warm without additional weight, you need them. If you want to stroll about the city all day, choose clothes that will help you stay dry by wicking away perspiration.

- Pack a few warm jackets or pullovers to put over your thermal foundation. Fabric and wool materials are great for warding off the cold.

- A well-made, thick winter coat is essential. Select a cushioned, waterproof item to shield you from wind, weather, and unexpected snowfall. To stroll a lot, a coat with a hood will provide additional weather protection.

- A scarf, hat, and gloves are three little and effective accessories that will keep you warm. Wearing padded gloves is essential to keep your hands warm while exploring; a thick scarf to cover your face and neck to block the wind is also recommended. A hat or cap with ear protection will keep your head warm.

- Wearing footwear that supports your feet is vital since they will be working hard throughout your stay. You'll need warm, weather-appropriate shoes since you'll be strolling on icy roads and slushy streets throughout the city's winter months.

- In a New York winter, good waterproof footwear is your best friend. Choose boots with adequate traction to prevent slipping on icy roadways, and make sure the padding keeps your feet toasty.

- Pack many pairs of socks that are both cooling and toasty. Wool socks are a wonderful option if your boots get a little wet since they keep your feet toasty, dry, and comfortable.

- If you intend to spend time indoors in moderate weather, you can also wish to bring along a pair of comfortable soft shoes for those instances when enormous boots aren't required.

To make sure you're prepared for everything that the New York winter may throw at you, you'll need a few items in addition to heavy clothing.

- Rain or snow could fall unexpectedly, so it's a sensible idea to take a compact, windproof umbrella. Pick one that is robust enough to withstand severe gusts and compact enough to fit in your baggage.

- Hand warmers, whether reusable or disposable, have to be on your winter purchasing list. On chilly days, you can tuck them inside your gloves or backpacks to give a little extra warmth.

- The cold, dry air can cause damage to your lips and cheeks. Take a good lip balm and a travel-sized lotion with you.

After spending the day exploring, you'll want to unwind in elegance. It's a beneficial idea to pack a few items that will help you relax and get ready for the following day's activities.

- Bring cozy loungewear or pajamas so you can relax in your hotel room after a long day. Anything warm and comfortable, like fleece or flannel, will feel amazing after spending time outdoors in the bitter weather.

- Include a pair of indoor shoes in your luggage if there is space. After walking around in heavy boots for the whole day, your feet will be grateful for the comfort.

Given that winters can be unpredictable, it's also good to prepare for the unexpected. Keeping a few extras in your backpack will help you handle any unforeseen circumstances.

- If all the walking has left you with burns, a basic first aid pack filled with bandages, painkillers, and any personal medications can just be the difference between wellness

- Carry a few small snacks, like granola bars or almonds, to sustain your energy levels while you're out and about. Plus, you can do this if you don't want to stop while exploring for a full supper.

- Bring some plastic or green shopping bags with you. They are handy for transporting other items, drying off damp garments, and preserving mementos you find along the route.

BUDGET FRIENDLY ACCOMMODATIONS

Selecting a fairly priced hotel is a terrific way to take in the charm of New York City over Christmas without going over budget. You can experience the festive spirit without compromising comfort thanks to these hotels, since they also offer cozy lodging in well-chosen settings:

- **Hotel 31**

For visitors on a budget, Hotel 31 is a wonderful option that offers a genuine taste of New York in a distinctive combination of affordability, elegance, and comfort. Tucked away at **120 E 31st St Apartment 7, New York, NY 10016**, this little hotel is conveniently close to popular places like Herald Square and the Empire State Building; just three blocks from the subway. The neighborhood is calm and peaceful, and it has many restaurants, shops, and entertainment options. When necessary, visitors can escape the bustle of the city thanks to Hotel 31's serene atmosphere. The hotel has well-designed rooms with cozy furnishings composed of antique hardwoods. Standard amenities in every accommodation include cable TV, safes, and free Wi-Fi. While some of the rooms include communal toilets, some have private bathrooms. Everything is kept immaculate by the housekeeping team. Hotel 31 is a fantastic deal, with nightly rates starting at $113 per person. Excellent attention is guaranteed for visitors at all times of the day with a 24-hour welcome.

- **Hotel Edison**

Perfectly located at **228 W 47th St., New York, NY 10036**, Hotel Edison is a renowned art deco masterpiece that dates back to 1931. Situated within a five-minute stroll from the Times Square-42nd Street metro station, this chic hotel offers superb accessibility to several prominent locations in New York, including the Empire State Building and Radio City Music Hall. Being near rail lines that allow you to explore the rest of the city is a convenient feature that makes this perfect for enjoying the thrill of Times Square. After a day of exploring, the rooms at Hotel Edison offer a sleek and pleasant sanctuary that mixes historic style with contemporary amenities. Benefits offered to visitors include flat-screen TVs, complimentary Wi-Fi, coffee makers, iPod docks, and designer bedding. For more space, the hotel provides apartments with various living areas; some have gardens, minibars, and breathtaking city views.

A complimentary wine hour is one way Hotel Edison enhances your stay and guest experience. It's a well-rounded option, with other attractions including a grand hall, a straightforward American diner, a two-story Italian restaurant, and a well-known drinking club. Excellent service, a convenient location, and a fascinating history make the Hotel Edison a memorable place to stay with rates starting at $165 per night, there are additional construction fees.

- **Pod 51**

Pod 51 is located at **230 E 51st St., New York, NY 10022**, and is a wonderful option for those seeking affordable accommodation that is both fashionable and functional. Situated  on a green block, this contemporary hotel is 1.1 miles from Times Square, giving it an ideal starting place for exploring the city. The well-designed, vivid rooms at Pod 51 have flat-screen TVs, iPod docks, complimentary Wi-Fi, workstations, and comfortable seating areas.

The variety of housing options caters to different requirements; some have private bathrooms, while others have access to common amenities. For visitors traveling in groups or on a budget, bunk bed rooms are a practical and affordable choice that nevertheless maintains comfort. Pod 51 differentiates itself from other budget-friendly motels by giving unique amenities that enrich the visitor experience. The year-round garden café provides a peaceful setting for a meal or coffee, while the eccentric lounge, complete with games and a bar, offers a vibrant gathering space. One of the hotel's greatest features is without a doubt its furnished rooftop terrace, where visitors can unwind and take in breathtaking city views. Thanks to where it is situated, excellent for easy access to metro stations, seeing the city's main attractions is made easier. Prices begin at $68 per night, a fair price considering the locale and facilities supplied.

- **Arlo NoMad**

 Located in the bustling NoMad neighborhood of Manhattan at **11 E 31st St., New York, NY 10016**, Arlo NoMad offers stylish and contemporary living that blends comfort with adventure. This hotel is a fantastic deal for travelers looking to explore the heart of New York City, with nightly rates from $199. The hotel rooms are a touch tiny, but that makes them ideal for lone travelers or couples since they are designed to maximize comfort and space. What distinguishes Arlo NoMad is the exceptional service provided by its personnel, who go above and beyond to ensure

visitors have a delightful stay. When you arrive, there's a level of attention to detail that elevates the whole experience, like a complimentary floor upgrade, an early check-in, or little touches like birthday cookies on special occasions. Arlo NoMad also offers other unique amenities that enhance the urban experience. When the weather permits, the rooftop bar is a must-visit because, while seasonal, it gives breathtaking views of the city skyline. The second-floor space with plenty of seating and tables, is a terrific spot to relax, more so when the rooftop is closed. With many dining and entertainment choices just a short stroll away, the hotel is in a perfect location for experiencing the city. The on-site café opens early and provides wonderful coffee and pastries to start the day, and guests get complimentary drinking water and a $15 ticket for the hotel's restaurant.

- **HI New York City Hostel**

The Hi New York City Hostel, housed in a gorgeous Victorian-style building on the Upper West Side at **891 Amsterdam Ave., New York, NY 10025**, is a great spot to start seeing the city. Located only a quick 13-minute walk from Columbia University and a 10-minute walk from Central Park, this hostel is in

 a bustling and handy area. Budget travelers will find the bright, bunk bed-equipped rooms with communal bathrooms, free WiFi, and enough light to suit their needs. The self-catering kitchen, gaming and TV rooms, subterranean patio, and garden, as well as other amenities, are all designed to make your stay at the hostel more pleasurable. The hostel offers a vibrant atmosphere ideal for meeting other guests and getting into the vacation spirit with its regular fun hours and organized evenings out. The availability of bike rentals is one of the things that provides an extra way to see the city. The hostel has a well-kept kitchen, comfortable common areas, and an energetic social scene, but keep in mind that not everything will appeal to everyone because it's a hostel.

- **The Local NY**

The Local NY is a stylish and cost-effective option for a contemporary, energetic hotel stay. Located at **13-02 44th Ave, Queens, NY 11101**, the chic hostel is just a short 4-minute walk from the nearest

metro station and 9 minutes' walk from the MoMA PS1 contemporary art exhibition. With breathtaking views of the Manhattan skyline, it is located in a beautifully restored industrial structure. Guests can select from basic mixed-and single-sex rooms with reading lights, bunk bed lockers, private bathrooms, and free WiFi. Separate rooms are also available for individuals who would like a bit more comfort and solitude. Among the many appealing elements of the hostel are an industrial chic bar and café, coin-operated laundry facilities, and a common kitchen. For many, the rooftop terrace is the main attraction because it provides a tranquil spot to relax and a breathtaking view of the city. Plus, The Local NY organizes many social gatherings that are perfect for establishing connections with other travelers.

- **American Dream Bed and Breakfast**

The American Dream Bed & Breakfast is located in

 the lovely Gramercy Park neighborhood in the heart of New York City and provides comfortable lodging at an affordable price. Located at **168 E 24th St., New York, NY 10010**, the family-run hostel offers convenient access to numerous major city landmarks. It is less than a mile from the renowned Empire State Building and a 4-minute walk from the 23rd Street train station. Bunk beds, TVs, and in-room sinks are provided in the rooms; shared amenities are also provided. Up to three people can stay in the rooms. Guests will find the fully equipped kitchen and spacious dining area to be useful, and they will get complimentary breakfast every morning while they stay.

Adding to providing comfortable and tidy rooms, American Dream Bed & Breakfast has a range of services to enhance the guest experience. Basic needs are met by the coin-operated laundry facilities and business center, and cooking is made simple in the common kitchen. The beautiful setting of the hotel is complemented by the attentive and enthusiastic personnel, who make sure that every visitor feels calm.

- **The Historic Blue Moon Hotel**

 Situated in the Lower East Side at **100 Orchard St., New York, NY 10002**, the Historic Blue Moon Hotel has a delightful blend of contemporary elegance and architectural splendor. This compact hotel, located in a superbly restored 19th-century apartment building, is conveniently close to SoHo's commercial district and the metro, just two streets away. It takes roughly seven minutes to walk there. The hotel's distinctive ambiance is further boosted by the original building elements, like marble flooring and antique light fixtures that will impress. The rooms are stylishly designed with warm hues and nostalgic accents and are equipped with high-thread-count bedding, iPod docks, minifridges, and free WiFi. For guests seeking extra luxury, upgraded guest rooms with private living areas, hydromassage tubs, terraces, and tall

ceilings are perfect. The Historic Blue Moon Hotel provides a range of thoughtful amenities to ensure that visitors have a comfortable and enjoyable stay. To start the day off right, a complimentary buffet breakfast with freshly baked cookies and bagels is provided every day. In an effort to enhance the stay, the hotel provides complimentary wine upon arrival and passes to a neighboring fitness center.

NYC'S CHRISTMAS SPECTACLES

Exploring the Christmas Spectacles in New York is a magical experience, as the city is turned into a snowy wonderland with twinkling lights, festive music, and joyous celebration, the city's dazzling Christmas lights, famous landmarks, and joyous festivities will captivate you.

❖ **Rockefeller Center's Christmas Tree**

The Rockefeller Center situated at **45 Rockefeller Plaza, New York, NY 10111**, is renowned for its festive Christmas events. Every year, the area is transformed into a mystical place, with the tall Rockefeller Center Christmas Tree serving as the focal point. This spectacular highlight has been a New York tradition since 1931 and is a well-known representation of the holiday season. The tree, often a Norway spruce, is covered with thousands of flashing lights, and a stunning Swarovski star is fastened to the top, creating an incredible sight that attracts visitors from all over. When the formal start of Christmas in New York occurs in late November or early December, a large crowd gathers to see the lighting spectacle. The tree's surroundings are equally fascinating. The rink below is modest and lovely, with a typical New York ice skating experience. Glide across the ice at Rockefeller Center and enjoy a unique skating experience against a backdrop of a gorgeous tree and vibrant lights. The rink is often crowded, but its unique appeal stems from the Christmas lights and music that enhance its vintage New York ambience.

The Rockefeller Center complex has a rich history and is aesthetically pleasing, with a total of 19 commercial buildings. Its Art Deco design elements have been modernized and preserved with care. One of the views is the Top of the Rock Observation Deck, situated on the 70th level of 30 Rockefeller Plaza. Visitors will enjoy expansive views of the city from here, and these are particularly lovely during the holidays when the city is illuminated by glittering lights. The observation platform provides a distinctive perspective of the tree and the surrounding Christmas décor from above. In addition to the rink and tree, Rockefeller Center is home to several additional structures and attractions. The iconic Radio City Music Hall, site of the annual Radio City Christmas Spectacular that features a stunning holiday performance by the well-known Rockettes, is only a short walk away. The area is a great spot to dine and shop during the holidays since it is surrounded by many restaurants and shops.

- Explore more than 100 well-known locations and retail stores where visitors can enjoy delicious food and unique merchandise. The layout of the complex makes it possible for visitors to explore the many artistic and cultural components included in its historic structures.

- The buildings around Rockefeller Center, such as the NBC Studios' renowned Art Deco towers and the Rainbow Room, an opulent dining establishment with expansive city vistas, also showcase the center's cheerful splendor.

- The plaza's holiday decorations, which include poinsettias, wreaths, and Christmas lights, boost the overall experience by generating a pleasant mood that is perfect for both visitors and locals.

❖ **Macy's Winter Décor**

 During the holidays, Macy's, located at **151 W 34th St., New York, NY 10001,** transforms into a mystical paradise with its exquisite holiday windows, attracting both residents and visitors. Macy's with its flagship shop on 34th Street in Herald Square, decorates its window with a whimsical and joyful display this time of year. And these Holiday Windows are a treasured New York institution that has delighted visitors of all ages for many years. The exterior is decked up with festive decorations and dazzling lights that create a welcoming atmosphere as you approach. Every year, Macy's modifies the subject of their windows in order to effectively depict people and tales from well-known stories. Christmastime brings with it an abundance of

detailed patterns, vivid hues, and animated displays that evoke feelings of wonder and nostalgia. Families and visitors alike assemble in front of the windows to take in the intricate details and fine craftsmanship. In and of itself, Macy's is worth a visit around the holidays. In the eight-story shop, there are many different types of clothing, household products, beauty products, accessories, and other items. Inside will greet visitors with a bustling, energetic atmosphere. The inside is decked up in festive décor, and the renowned wooden escalators; a nod to the store's history complete the atmosphere.

It's a one-stop shop that caters to all of your Christmas shopping requirements, offering unusual holiday gifts plus brand apparel. Macy's is a wonderful spot to take a break from your shopping spree since it offers a variety of culinary options. There are alternatives for a leisurely supper or a quick snack, and the in-store restaurants complete the picture with a simple and pleasant dining experience. Macy's offers gift wrapping and monogramming services to customers wanting to add a personal touch to their holiday presents. The thought behind your gifts will be as treasured as the item itself. When visiting Macy's during the holidays, a trip to the top floor containing the store's Christmas area is an absolute must. With its assortment of Christmas décor, ornaments, wreaths, and associated dinnerware, this section is a veritable gold mine. There's nothing like the pure delight of taking in the wide diversity in this vibrant setting, even if some of it may feel familiar. Macy's is renowned for its participation in the Thanksgiving Day Parade, another New York City tradition that heralds the start of the holiday season. The procession concludes in front of Macy's Herald Square, contributing to the well-known significance of the business during the holidays. Giant balloons, floats, and marching bands are all part of the procession.

❖ **Bryant Park Winter Village**

Bryant Park Winter Village, located at **42nd Street and 6th Avenue, New York, NY 10018,** is another must-visit during Christmas. From Thanksgiving to New Year's, it is transformed into a breathtaking winter wonderland giving the perfect balance of seasonal activities, shopping, and relaxing in front of the city's iconic skyline. The Empire State

 Building serves as the backdrop for the stunning Winter Village that wonderfully embodies the spirit of the holidays. Winter Village's central attraction is the well-known ice skating rink. The large, free-to-enter rink in Bryant Park allows you to skate while taking in the twinkling holiday lights. Visitors can rent skating equipment on-site. A large Christmas tree encircles the rink, giving a magnificent atmosphere for skaters and bystanders alike.

Whatever your skill level, this rink is a wonderful place to enjoy a traditional winter sport. The Christmas lights in the park add to the festive atmosphere. There are many different Christmas retailers scattered around the charming, custom-built booths. The sellers of these enterprises are a varied bunch, offering unique gifts, handcrafted jewelry, and décor. Unique findings perfect for Christmas gifts are ensured by the emphasis on local small businesses and artists. The food and drink options are another essential part of visiting Bryant Park Winter Village. There are many food vendors throughout the park to satisfy any appetite. With selections for gourmet appetizers, desserts, and hot beverages to warm your hands, there is something to suit every taste. The food vendors give a wonderful chance to sample local cuisine and enjoy the vibrant atmosphere. Bryant Park Winter Village, in addition to skating and stores, presents a range of events and activities to add to the festive ambiance. Love visitors and families will love the vibrant and dynamic environment created by the regular live music events, seminars, and special events. Bryant Park is transformed into a whole Christmas experience when these activities are combined. The fact that the park is easily accessible by public transportation in the heart of Manhattan makes it even more desirable.

❖ Dyker Heights Christmas Lights

The Dyker Heights Christmas Lights experience brilliantly captures the essence of the lovely New York holidays. This neighborhood located at **1072 80th St., 1st Floor, Brooklyn, NY 11228**, is well-known for its lavish events and attracts

 thousands of visitors each year who are in awe of the breathtaking displays. Dyker Heights comes to life with lights, decorations, and a cheery atmosphere during the Christmas season, and should be on everyone's itinerary. Dyker Heights is unique because of the community's commitment to elegantly and generously celebrating the changing of the seasons. The neighborhood is well-known for its immaculate homes, many featuring exquisite Christmas décor, including nativity scenes, reindeer, and life-size Santa Claus statues, in addition to shimmering lights.

The most well-known homes have elaborate décor, particularly those located on 84th, 85th, and 11th Avenues. The best way to see the attractions of this paradise for those who like to explore it is with a guided tour. DHCL (Dyker Heights Christmas Lights), a fantastic tour that immerses visitors in the atmosphere of the season, is run by residents.

The journey begins with a convenient pickup in Manhattan's Bryant Park, not far from the Winter Village. When visitors arrive at Dyker Heights, they are taken on a walking tour of the top viewing locations in the region after enjoying a pleasant drive with an informative tour guide. This walking tour will allow visitors to fully appreciate the intricate workmanship and extensive expanse of the decorations.

Visitors will enjoy the festive atmosphere as they cruise the streets with hot chocolate in hand, taking in the magnificent lights and joyous decorations. Even while the tour makes sure you don't miss any of the must-see residences, taking your time exploring Dyker Heights is just as much fun. It's wonderful to visit Dyker Heights between 5:00 and 9:00 p.m., when the lights are at their peak. Weekends are even more enjoyable since everyone is decked out in their finest holiday attire and there are even more lights across the neighborhood. The experience is enhanced by the area itself. With its well-manicured fields, streets lined with trees, and a strong sense of community shown by the way neighbors collaborate to put on this annual event.

But it's crucial that you thoroughly plan your travels. Parking in Dyker Heights will be tough during the busy Christmas season, so it's best to park a few streets away and walk to the main attractions. Guests should allow enough time for their exploration since the region is fairly far from Manhattan; if traveling from the city, allow around 90 minutes for each way. When you get there, plan on spending at least 1.5 to 2 hours exploring the lights and taking photographs to ensure you see everything.

❖ **Union Square Holiday Market**

 Nestled at **E 14th St., New York, NY 10011**, in the bustling Union Square Park, the Union Square Holiday Market captivates all with its astounding array of holiday experiences each year. This winter wonderland is a must-see, open from late October to January 2. It has more than 150 outdoor stores with a distinctive assortment of excellent dining, home furnishings, art, and crafts. The Union Square

Holiday Market's extraordinary range of one-of-a-kind and handcrafted products is one of its charms. The market is a treasure trove for finding extraordinary and one-of-a-kind gifts; it offers exquisitely created jewelry, pottery, original artwork, and home décor. Locally made goods are on display at many booths, giving a wonderful opportunity to support small businesses and local artists. The Union Square Holiday Market is renowned for its extensive and mouthwatering food selection, in addition to its shopping.

The market is a visual feast, with an array of food kiosks and pop-ups selling gourmet treats and international street cuisine. The aroma of freshly cooked sausages permeates the air at the popular German Bratwurst stand. The bratwurst is a must-try when it's served warm on a bun with sauerkraut and mustard for anyone craving something bold and spicy. Other eating delights include truffle fries, gourmet hot cocoa, and a variety of sweet and spicy delicacies. It is crucial to exercise patience since wait times can lengthen, more so for well-known products. Nevertheless, the city's best festive treats are worth the wait. The

Union Square Holiday Market is a joyous occasion that wonderfully captures the splendor of the year. The wonderfully adorned market stalls, together with the shimmering lights and seasonal décor that surround the park, create a warm and inviting atmosphere. An extra element of enchantment is given to the experience when visiting the market in the evening when the lights are gleaming. The market's convenient location in the heart of Union Square makes it simple to get to, and its vibrant atmosphere; complete with live music and street performers, makes it a wonderful way to celebrate the season.

- For the best experience, visit in the evening when the Christmas lights are at their most magnificent. Particularly on weekends and during the peak shopping hours, be ready for crowds.

- Popular food items can generate long lines, so be prepared to wait in line. To avoid the longest lines, try arriving at less busy times or visiting other food vendors.

- Wear comfortable shoes because there will be a lot of walking. As there may not be as many services as you would want at the market, it's also a beneficial idea to use the restroom beforehand.

- At your leisure, browse the many distinct vendors. There will be something for everyone to find what they want.

❖ **Holiday Train Show, NYBG**

 A popular holiday tradition, the Holiday Train Show at the New York Botanical Garden **(2900 Southern Blvd., Bronx, NY 10458)** enthralls visitors with its lovely display of little trains and well-crafted architectural models. This festive event that takes place against the stunning backdrop of the garden's natural beauty, is a delightful blend of Christmas cheer and thoughtful innovation. The Holiday Train Show's major attraction is its magnificent collection of model trains that go

through an outstanding set of scale replicas of well-known New York locations. Each year, it features new and contemporary exhibits that draw attention to the stunning architecture of well-known buildings, bridges, and historical places. Pinecones, sticks, and leaves are just a few of the natural elements used to craft each item with care. The presentation has a remarkable amount of detail that adds a unique touch of artistry and recollection.

With an amazing approach across a gorgeously decorated field, the stage is set for the festive joy that lies ahead. You'll witness a range of trains passing by remarkably accurate pictures of famous New York City places as you visit the exhibit. Every structure, including the Statue of Liberty and the Empire State Building, is a testament to the creativity and expertise that go into this annual celebration. Giving an entertaining and captivating experience for all ages is the aim of the Holiday Train Show. Both kids and adults will love the interactive elements, including trains that can be operated by buttons for more excitement. A treasure hunt that motivates kids to explore and look for hidden jewels within the exhibit enhances their experiences even more. The spectacle is also a multi-sensory experience. The garden is illuminated with vibrant lights from the outdoor glow-light display as evening approaches, lending a mystical touch and a captivating atmosphere. Since the event lasts for many weeks, there is enough opportunity to enjoy the exhibit at your pace.

- To avoid large crowds, plan for visiting after the busiest holiday season. Since tickets are timed to regulate admission and give a positive experience, be sure to make reservations in advance.

- Parking is available on-site for a fee, and there is free street parking nearby. You can guarantee a spot and have a more relaxed start to your vacation if you arrive early.

- Wear comfortable shoes, as exploring the exhibit in its entirety may take up to 1.5 hours. There are paths leading to other parts of the garden, make sure you stay on the main track to properly experience the train display. The performance gets underway outdoors.

- There are reasonably priced food stands where you can get a bite to eat while enjoying the cheerful atmosphere.

- Participate in the kid- and adult-friendly treasure hunt for an additional thrill and interaction.

❖ **The Radio City Christmas Spectacular**

The annual Radio City Christmas Special, held at the renowned Radio City Music Hall, is one of the highlights of the holiday in New York. It is a wonderful occasion well-known for its magnificent performers, lovely surroundings, and happy tradition that wonderfully captures the essence of Christmas. The magnificent edifice known as Radio City Music Hall, or the "Showplace of the Nation," is situated in the center of Manhattan at **1260 6th Ave., New York, NY 10020.** Constructed in 1932, this magnificent art deco theater has a beautiful interior replete with intricate details and astute architectural elements that transport patrons to another era. The theater's opulence creates a feeling that leaves the holidays unforgettable. The

iconic Radio City Rockettes are the star of the annual Christmas extravaganza and are none other than the legendary Radio City Rockettes. These dancers are well-known for their timing and precision, bringing an exciting Christmas performance to life. The act's highlights are their incredible dancing and signature high-kick moments that leave spectators in disbelief. A delightful event, the Christmas Spectacular features amazing dance routines, captivating narrative, and traditional holiday music.

Highlights of the production include a genuine Nativity scene, a visit from Santa Claus, and a superb orchestra that brings the singing portions to life. The elaborate stage designs and striking costume changes add to the overall attractiveness of the presentation.

- Christmas spectacular tickets tend to sell out quickly, so it's vital to get them well in advance. Doors open one hour before the performance, giving you plenty of time to choose a spot and get comfortable before the acts begin, which start at about 4 PM.

- Arrive at least one hour before showtime to guarantee a smooth security check and avoid lengthy waits. The venue's fast and simple security procedures are designed to resemble airport security inspections.

- The Radio City Music Hall is renowned for having comfortable chairs and a tidy environment. The restrooms are spotless, and the lines move swiftly. There are also food and drink concessions; while the prices may be a touch high, the experience is worthwhile.

ELEMENTARY HOLIDAY ATTRACTIONS

Affordable Skating Rinks for Ice Skating Under the Stars

Enjoy the pleasures of ice skating in New York City without exceeding your budget. And here we'll go over few of the best affordable rinks where you can skate in a fun environment;

- **Wollman Rink**

With a breathtaking view of New York City's skyline, Wollman Rink, located at **Q29G+46, 830 5th Ave, New York, NY 10065**, presents an excellent ice skating experience, accessible every day from 10 a.m., and has been a cornerstone of New York City's winter celebrations for more than 70 years. As you skate on the ice at Wollman Rink, you'll be treated to breathtaking views of Central Park and the surrounding area.

Your skating experience will be enhanced by the rink's surroundings having a stunning view of Manhattan. With a warm and inviting atmosphere for everyone, the Wollman Park Partners-managed rink is dedicated to fostering cultural celebration and community interaction. The entrance fee to Wollman Rink is $6 per person. Because of its popularity, it's advisable to purchase tickets online in advance, particularly during the hectic holiday season. Even with timed tickets, it's still advised to arrive a bit early to avoid any lineups and secure your spot; this will help you organize your visit and cut down on wait times.

There is plenty of room for skaters to have fun on the large rink. During peak season, longer lineups are anticipated; but, they usually move quickly. If you visit the rink during off-peak hours, there won't be much of a wait. The rink has lockers for a modest fee, making it simple to keep personal items while you skate. Wollman Rink offers a more relaxed, less crowded skating experience without the hectic atmosphere. Families and groups looking to enjoy a traditional winter pastime in one of New

York's most picturesque settings will find this venue perfect.

- Purchase your tickets online to avoid standing in line. Aim to be at the skating spot at least half an hour early.

- To keep your personal belongings secure, budget an additional $7 for lockers.

- Skate rentals are available at the rink if you don't have yours.

- A variety of hot beverages and snacks are available from on-site food vendors.

- **The Rink At Rockefeller Center**

A typical New York experience is visiting The Rink at **600 5th Avenue, Rockefeller Center, New York, NY 10020,** particularly in the winter months. Tickets for this annual ice skating rink start at $32 per person, providing a fantastic experience among the vibrant energy of Manhattan. This rink, set against the iconic backdrop of the Prometheus monument and the towering Rockefeller Center Christmas Tree, transforms into a magnificent winter wonderland  that embodies the spirit of Christmas in the heart of the city. The Rink at Rockefeller Center, one of the world's most famous ice skating rinks, has come to represent festive times in New York during Christmas. Open daily, skaters of all ages are invited to enjoy the happy atmosphere that only Rockefeller Center can offer as they glide on the ice's smooth surface. The Christmas Tree, adorned with hundreds of shimmering lights, rises above you, giving the impression that you've walked into a holiday postcard for every second spent on the ice.

A touch of elegance and history is added to the encounter by the golden Prometheus figure that lords over the setting. The rink is smaller, more intimate and private than other rinks in the city. It also doesn't really matter whether this is your first time skating or you have a lot of experience; taking a skate lesson in this well-known location is something unique. Everyone should at least feel the exhilaration of sliding on this timeless ice. The rink has hosted numerous events for visitors from around the world. To maximize your visit to The Rink at Rockefeller Center, especially during the busy Christmas season, buy tickets in advance. By doing this, you can ensure that you obtain a spot on the ice and cut down on waiting time. It's also a beneficial idea to arrive early so you have time to register, rent skates if needed, and enjoy the surroundings before you hit the ice.

While you skate on the tidy rink, you can keep your belongings in the locker rooms. A flawless experience from start to finish is enhanced by the staff's promptness and kindness. The Rink at Rockefeller Center is special because of the atmosphere it fosters, not because of its location or history. While skating, you'll be surrounded by the sights and sounds of New York during the most picturesque season of the year. The joyful music, colorful décor, and overall sense of community all enhance the occasion. It's a place where enduring memories are created and where the magic of Christmas comes to life on the ice.

• The ice rink in Bryant Park

 One of New York City's most lovely Christmas places is the Bryant Park Ice Rink, featuring a stunning winter experience amid the city's dynamic energy. Bryant Park, a beloved winter haven, is situated in the heart of Manhattan, at **New York, NY 10018**, adjacent to the famous New York Public Library. It is well-known for its ice skating rink. This vibrant rink is free to enter and is among the least expensive ways to celebrate the holidays.

During the holidays, Bryant Park welcomes you with gorgeous landscape that appears like it may be seen in a photograph. Slide across the ice in front of a breathtaking backdrop of the park's surrounding structures. Nestled within the verdant parklands, the rink enhances the whole experience and is a must-visit. The park is open daily from 7 a.m. until 11 p.m., giving visitors plenty of opportunities to take in the upbeat atmosphere. Skaters of all experience levels are welcome to use the rink, regardless of ability level. If you reserve a time slot online and bring your skates, you can use the rink for free. If not, skates are reasonably priced and can be rented. One of Bryant Park Ice Rink's attractions is the nearby Winter Village, where over a hundred merchants set up shop and offer delectable snacks and handcrafted goods. This enhances the enjoyment element of your skating experience by letting you browse exclusive Christmas merchandise or savor delectable snacks and beverages in between skate sessions. The Lodge is an indoor seating area next to the rink, providing a comfortable retreat for a filling meal or drink.

Kids will find the Bryant Park Ice Rink to be a very appealing place. With the park's selection of assisted skating devices, even the youngest visitors can enjoy the ice safely and the staff is ready to help skaters of all ages. There is enough seating available surrounding the rink for non-skaters to unwind and take in a fantastic vantage point of the action. Beyond the rink, Bryant Park is a popular destination all year round because of its captivating cultural events, cost-free activities, and lovely landscapes. In the winter months, the park really embodies the essence of the winter season. The Bryant Park Ice Rink in the heart of New York City offers a distinctive Christmas experience with its twinkling lights and lovely holiday music playing.

Joyous Views from The Top

There's nothing like seeing New York from above, mostly during the winter. Distinguished places are done out in their festive finest, and the city is converted into a beautiful patchwork of lights. When seen from above, the city appears to be teeming with Christmas cheer, with the streets below decked out in twinkling lights and a joyous atmosphere. The beauty of the enormous Christmas tree at Rockefeller Center, the illuminated bridges, and the brightly colored buildings will not be missed. These images capture the essence of a New York Christmas, where the cityscape and holiday traditions blend together beautifully.

The best way to enjoy the holidays is to take in these Christmas sights from above. You can really take in all of New York's vitality and beauty at this most wonderful time of year, which is a time for reflection and relaxation. Here are a few modestly priced sites in New York where you can take in the festive vistas from the top during Christmas:

- **Top of the Rock**

 Over the holidays, there's nowhere better than the Top of the Rock to take in the breathtaking winter scenery of New York. Perched 70 storeys above the city, the Top of the Rock Observation Deck at **30 Rockefeller Plaza, New York, NY 10112**, gives unparalleled 360-degree views. At the start of the tour, you take a pleasant elevator to the observation levels, where you can explore three different viewing places, each with a certain charm of its own.

The first level has both indoor and outdoor observation areas that are excellent for weather-related sightseeing. Step outside and you're greeted with expansive views of Central Park, the Empire State Building, and Manhattan's breathtaking surroundings. The second story has a large outside terrace with even better views of the city below. The huge vistas go well beyond the local region, including views of the Hudson River, the Statue of Liberty, and the shimmering lights of the bridges that connect Manhattan with the distant cities. In the end, the top deck presents the greatest view, letting you fully appreciate the magnificence and majesty of New York City. With the 360-degree view, you can see the city from every direction and enjoy a range of breathtaking vistas. This fantastic event is made much more spectacular by Christmas. The iconic Rockefeller Center Christmas Tree rising just below, adds a touch of seasonal enchantment to the already breathtaking vista as it twinkles with festive lights all over.

A once-in-a-lifetime opportunity to see the city bathed in winter sunlight by day or at night as it twinkles with Christmas lights is provided by The Top of the Rock. For those who want to visit New York during its most picturesque time of year, this excursion is a must-do, with tickets beginning at $33 per person. The staff at Top of the Rock ensures a seamless and enjoyable stay from the time you arrive until you go, freeing you to concentrate on enjoying the breathtaking views and creating enduring memories.

- **One World Observatory**

Perched atop the highest building in the Western Hemisphere, One World Observatory **(117 West St., New York, NY 10007)** offers a spectacular tour of the heart of New York City, especially beautiful around Christmas. Situated on the 100th and 102nd stories of the renowned One World Trade Center, the telescope spans over 125,000 square feet and provides a unique viewing experience that blends creativity and imagination.

Your experience begins with a thrilling ride in the SkyPod Elevator. The city's skyline unfolds before you as you ascend, altered by decades of building construction. The real magic begins when you reach level 100 and are whisked away in just a minute. Gorgeous 360-degree views that stretch up to 45 kilometers in all directions will be all around you once you reach the peak. Three of the most well-known sights in the city; the Statue of Liberty, the Brooklyn Bridge, and the Empire State Building, can all be seen from an incredible new perspective. The observatory is even more stunning during the holidays. This must-visit spot is enhanced by the festive attitude that elevates the already breathtaking vistas, making it the perfect place for feeling the Christmas spirit from the best viewing point in the city. Imagine looking up at the iconic Manhattan skyline as it twinkles. The seasonal decorations of the observatory add a touch of Christmas cheer to your visit. For individuals with a strong sense of optimism and nostalgia for the original Twin Towers, a trip to One World Observatory will be an inspiring experience.

The region aims to honor the past while also showcasing New York's resiliency and future. It's an inspiring and poignant trip that adds depth to the breathtaking visual experience. Beyond the vistas, the tower has many exhibits showcasing One World Trade Center's and New York's remarkable histories. After admiring the views, you can visit these informative displays or dine at one of the observatory's dining options. Food packages are handed out with the purchase of a ticket, offering a convenient way to enjoy a festive meal outdoors.

One World Observatory's regular hours are 9 AM to 9 PM, so you have plenty of time to plan your visit. It is a reasonably priced vacation, starting at $32 per person. To maximize your trip, especially during the holidays, book your tickets in advance. You may also think about purchasing a priority ticket in order to skip the lineups and spend as much time as possible admiring the views.

- **Edge**

The Edge, situated at **30 Hudson Yards, New York, NY 10001**, really lives up to its name. From this cutting-edge viewing platform, visitors can get a whole new perspective on the city. Before heading out onto The Edge, visitors are given a preview of what's to come. The opening's interactive exhibits give an intriguing look at future city design while also evoking the creative spirit that defines it. This glimpse into the future perfectly predicts the adventure that awaits; a voyage beyond the realm of the possible. Perched 1,131 feet above the bustling streets of Manhattan, The Edge provides one of the most breathtaking views. Reaching the hundredth level of 30 Hudson Yards, the observation deck presents a unique perspective where you can look into the sky and gaze down through a glass floor at the city below. The expansive 360-degree views are a sight to see, particularly at dusk, and span from the renowned Midtown buildings to the shimmering Hudson River waters.

As day gives way to night, New York City's Christmas lights twinkle, creating a captivating, almost surreal setting. While standing on The Edge, seeing the city lights come to life beneath you as the sun sets is an incredible experience that perfectly captures the essence of the season. Remember to bring warm clothes while visiting The Edge during the holiday. The whole observation platform is outside, and it will become chilly as winter closes in. Remember to bring an additional jacket, gloves, and a scarf so you can stay warm while taking in the breathtaking scenery. Because

The Edge is so well-known, wait times are often quite lengthy. To guarantee a more seamless experience, it is advisable to purchase your tickets in advance. In addition to its breathtaking vistas, The Edge provides extra facilities for individuals who want to enhance their experience even further. At the rooftop bar, you can choose from a wide selection of drinks while taking in city views and enjoying a beverage. In order to obtain a breathtaking view of the city below, thrill-seekers may even lean out over the edge at a secure spot. Ideal for those seeking a spike in energy. Enjoy the more relaxed atmosphere by sitting on the outdoor stairs and taking in the view. Following your visit to The Edge, the area offers a plethora of dining, shopping, and exploration options, such as The Vessel and the Hudson Yards boutiques.

- **Brooklyn Heights Promenade**

The lesser-known Brooklyn Heights Promenade offers breathtaking views of some of the most well-known places in New York City. It is nestled away at **Montague St. & Pierrepont Pl., Brooklyn, NY 11201**. Open daily from 6 AM to 1 AM, this tree-lined promenade is the perfect spot to embrace the beauty and serenity of the  surroundings and get into the holiday spirit. The nicest thing is that it's free to visit. The Statue of Liberty, the Brooklyn Bridge, and Manhattan City are all visible from the 1,826-foot-long Brooklyn Heights Promenade. The promenade is even more charming in the winter months. The Statue of Liberty rising over the glittering city lights in the distance is a really amazing sight. The holiday lights on the Brooklyn Bridge enhance its allure and create a scene straight out of a holiday postcard.

The beach offers a unique sensation that cannot be duplicated, day or night. The serene sidewalk image is starkly contrasted with the bustling bustle of New York City's waterways during the day. You can watch the boats float over the East River or see the iconic yellow taxis race across the Brooklyn Bridge. The crisp winter air and the vibrancy of the city invite an active walk. When the sun goes down, the promenade turns into a tranquil haven. The spectacular display created by the hundreds of lights that make up the Manhattan skyline is especially captivating during the holidays. The perfect setting for introspection, a memorable night, and soaking in the festive mood is created by the serene beauty of the night and the twinkling city lights. With the addition of lights and other holiday decorations, the walkway has a vibrant atmosphere during the holidays. Strolling down the path at this time of year is like stepping into a snow dream. There are festive displays and beautifully decorated Christmas trees nearby that add to the enchanted ambiance. A stroll down the Brooklyn Heights Promenade during the holidays is a unique experience. The combination of the crisp winter air, the sparkling lights of the Manhattan skyline, and the sporadic sound of carol singers in the distance creates an atmosphere of cheerful delight.

Historical Holiday Highlights

As Christmas approaches, New York becomes a stunning winter paradise, and the city's lengthy history just adds to the charm. Numerous inexpensive historical sites that encapsulate the spirit of the city's history can be explored all across the city. These places are ideal for visiting while taking in the festive ambiance of Christmas because they each give a distinctive look into New York City's past.

- **Federal Hall National Memorial**

A hidden treasure located at **26 Wall St., New York, NY 10005**. The Federal Hall National Memorial was the site of the first Congress meeting and the swearing-in ceremony for George Washington as the country's first president. Here were penned the Bill of Rights and some of the most significant discussions that helped to form the nation. The ceremony is being performed today even though this is the second building where these significant events took place. The current structure functions as both a monument and a museum. It is now a part of the United States and was originally used as

a customs house in 1842. You'll notice the enormous columns and remarkable similarities to historic temples like the Parthenon as you enter. This structure blends American history with neoclassical architecture. Visits to Federal Hall over the holidays evoke a special level of introspection and recollections. The museum is open daily from 10 AM to 5 PM on weekdays, offering a peaceful respite from the hectic streets of New York City.

It's a wonderful spot to visit for visitors interested in history or the origins of American democracy. The guided tours give profound insights into American history and are a fascinating experience; since admission is free. This facility has exhibits that tell the narrative of the site's evolution, from Washington's inauguration to its service as a Customs House and finally as a National Treasury. One of the highlights is the stone slab that George Washington stood on during his inauguration; it gives a tangible connection to a significant historical moment. The ancient structure is gone, but the atmosphere is still historical; mostly since you're walking on the same marble floors as the old entrepreneurs. Federal Hall has a serene aura throughout the winter, perfect for contemplating the nation's inception. The museum also hosts regular historical reenactments that engage visitors and bring the past to life. Spend some time learning about the significance of the events that took place inside these walls as you explore the museum: the first free speech discussions, the drafting of the Bill of Rights, and the inauguration of the country's first president. It's a poignant occasion that's made much more memorable by the festive spirit of Christmas, serving as a reminder of the ageless principles that shaped the nation and a bridge to the past.

- **St. Patrick's Cathedral**

Finished in 1879, St. Patrick's Cathedral is a towering Neo-Gothic treasure nestled at **5th Ave., New York, NY 10022**, a testament to faith, perseverance, and creative beauty. Millions of visitors from across the globe have visited this stunning chapel, situated just across Rockefeller Center on Fifth Avenue. It

provides a space for prayer, contemplation, and awe. St. Patrick's Cathedral becomes an incredible winter wonderland around Christmas, bolstered by festive decorations that bring emphasis to its already splendid interior. Beautiful stone carvings, majestic twin spires, and stained glass windows sparkle with additional warmth that beckons tourists into its serene embrace, even among the hustle and bustle of the city during the holidays.

All are invited to see the church's splendor; it opens daily at 6:45 AM. The Christmas Day service is one of the most cherished traditions observed at St. Patrick's during the holiday. With its candlelight and melodic music, the church interior offers a very spiritual experience that appeals to both religious and nonreligious people. When the Nativity scene is well constructed and presented, it draws a lot of attention and inspires hundreds of people to recognize its significance and intricacy. Despite the church's heavy visitation, particularly during the holidays, its expansive and beautiful grounds guarantee that there is always time for quiet reflection. Plus, St. Patrick's has a serene ambiance that allows visitors to unwind and appreciate the beauty of their surroundings, even in the heart of the bustle. Every aspect of the cathedral evokes wonder and contemplation, from the tall towers above to the exquisite altarpieces. Among them are the serene saint sculptures. There's much more to discover for those who decide to linger after the ceremony.

By purchasing presents and holy items from the cathedral's little store, you can carry a small piece of this well-known place home with you. And visitors can also remain to fully appreciate the artwork and architectural elements of the cathedral, since they are easy to overlook on a brief visit. Every statue and stained glass window of St. Patrick's tells a narrative, contributing to the church's unique religious and historical fabric. You should experience something more than just the building's physical attractiveness when you visit St. Patrick's Cathedral during the holiday. You should get an understanding of what makes this place so unique. Within the walls of one of the most recognizable structures in New York lies a journey through religion, art, and history. St. Patrick's Cathedral delivers a unique and transformative experience that lingers long after you leave its hallowed halls, making it an excellent destination regardless of your purpose for visiting. The greatest thing is that donations are always accepted and admission is free, helping to preserve this historical treasure for future generations. If you wish to explore the surrounding landmarks, it's simple to incorporate a visit to the church into your vacation itinerary. Located near Times Square and the Top of the Rock observation deck, it's a convenient and enjoyable stopover for your holiday travels in New York.

- **Trinity Church**
89 Broadway, New York, NY 10006 is home to the magnificent Trinity Church, a place where religion, history, and architectural beauty all come together. Since its founding in 1697, this well-known church has seen the transformation of New York from its earliest days as New Amsterdam to the bustling

metropolis it is today. It has endured as a symbol of

 perseverance and faith. Trinity Church has a special kind of appeal during Christmas. Inside, warmth and dignity abound, making it the perfect refuge from the winter chill and the hustle and bustle of the city. The spectacular altar, adorned with paintings and a stunning image of the Last Supper, is a major element of the church's interior. Upon arrival, guests are greeted by the magnificent sight of intricate stained glass windows that project vibrant patterns onto the stone walls.

The church's exquisite decorations that elevate its attractiveness even more, will stick in the minds of all that gets to see it for themselves. One of Trinity Church's most noteworthy aspects is its lengthy history that is intimately connected to the history of New York. The cemetery has some of the most well-known figures in American history. The bones of Alexander Hamilton, one of the founding fathers, as well as those of his wife Eliza and her sister

Angelica, rest here. Their graves, along with those of other notable New Yorkers like Robert Fulton and the lone signer of the Declaration of Independence buried in Manhattan, make for a powerful connection to the past. The church entrance includes a map pointing visitors to these significant locations. There are QR codes scattered across the grounds with further historical context. For those interested in history, Trinity Church is both a place of worship and a living museum that documents the city's founding history. The church was significant while the city was still known as New Amsterdam, as evidenced by its status as the biggest structure in New York at one time.

Surrounded by the towering Financial District skyscrapers, Trinity Church is a symbol of New York's resilient spirit to this day. The inside of the church offers a serene and contemplative environment that stands in stark contrast to the bustling streets outside. Everyone can benefit from Trinity Church's beautiful architecture, fascinating history, and opportunity to relax for a bit. The church's Christmas services are a joyous occasion, particularly with the beautiful organ music and festive décor. And even if you're not attending a service, just spending Christmas in this lovely environment will make you content and reflective. The grounds do shut in the evening, so it's a beneficial idea to verify the church's operating hours in advance. Trips in the early morning hours will be more peaceful and calm, letting you fully appreciate the beauty and tranquility of this sacred site.

- **New York Historical Society**

The New York Historical Society was established in 1804, is the city's oldest museum and brings with it a vibrant look into New York City's history via art, culture, and narratives. This vibrant museum, located on the West Side at **170 Central Park W, New York, NY 10024**, brings to life the colorful history of both America and New York via a range of exhibits, artifacts, and interactive experiences. The New York Historical Society becomes a delightful place as Christmas approaches, bringing festive color to the hallways that are already brimming with history. Visitors get a unique chance to learn about the history of the city associated with the holiday by seeing the Christmas decorations at the museum. The museum becomes a historical winter wonderland, replete with uniquely designed exhibits that delve into New York's past Christmas traditions and wonderfully decorated trees influenced by different historical periods. Christmas history programs often include themes that highlight the many ways that New Yorkers have observed the holiday over the years.

There could be exhibits detailing the development of Christmas decorations, gift-giving traditions, or even the city's contribution to the expansion of certain holiday rituals. These presentations are not only beautifully rendered and very instructive, but they also give context on the ways that New York has influenced and been influenced by Christmas customs across the globe. One of the museum's regular highlights is its exquisite display of Tiffany lights that is even more appealing around the holidays. The warm, cheerful atmosphere these gorgeous, brilliant lights generate makes them a must-see when you visit the museum. The Tiffany

Lamp Gallery is a breathtaking sight that wonderfully captures the beauty and brightness of the holidays with its illuminated staircase. Because of the museum's extensive collection, there are many study options available. A perennial favorite, the kids' section enthralls young minds with thought-provoking displays that make studying history an exciting adventure. Comprehensive exhibits at the New York Historical Society also chart the city's history from its founding as New Amsterdam to its ascent to prominence as a major global metropolis.

During the holidays, the museum may have special exhibitions that focus on the city's historical Christmases, giving these artifacts a new lease of life. One such program might illustrate how holiday rituals have developed from the Sinterklaas festivities of the Dutch settlers to the bustling, commercial Christmases of the 20th century. For those interested in political history, the White House Oval Office replica at the museum offers a fascinating glimpse into the former presidents who have impacted the nation. This famous program becomes even more significant during Christmas, serving as a reminder of the joyful and unifying national events that have taken place in that same office. The New York Historical Society is open every day from 11 a.m. to 5 p.m. (closed on Mondays) and has exhibitions spread over four levels. There is plenty of time for visitors to browse the exhibits. On Fridays, when admission is sometimes free in the evening, the museum is particularly welcoming.

- **The Tenement Museum**

The Tenement Museum, situated at **103 Orchard St., New York, NY 10002**, gives a unique view into the lives of the immigrants who formed the city and, subsequently, the nation. This historic institution, based in a refurbished 1863 apartment building, brings the experiences of working-class immigrants to reality with fascinating guided journeys. With a deeper comprehension of how immigrant families celebrated Christmas in their new country, the museum offers a special attraction throughout the holidays. The museum's Christmas tours give a poignant look into the struggles and victories of these families, who often had to overcome adversity while attempting to start over in a bustling, foreign city. The museum provides a variety of journeys to suit every interest, but during Christmas, the emphasis is on family traditions, seasonal rituals, and the resoluteness of these immigrant groups. You can experience the understated and meaningful ways these families celebrated Christmas, with simple decorations and banquets honoring customs from their former lives.

Plus highlighting the variations in Christmas customs across immigrant communities, these walks emphasize the universal themes of survival, hope, and family. The painstakingly restored apartments inside the former tenement building are available for exploration only on guided tours. These tours are interactive lecture series where educated instructors meticulously assemble the unique narratives of the individuals who formerly lived there. For instance, one can end up living in the modest apartment of an Irish immigrant family and seeing firsthand their struggles and strategies for preserving their cultural identity while adapting to American life. As an alternative, you can go inside a Jewish family's home and see how they celebrated Hanukkah despite facing many difficulties after moving to New York from Eastern Europe. The museum's instructors, who are experts in their fields, impart not only historical details but also the emotional context that imbues these stories with significance. Throughout the journey, guests are often able to share their stories, enhancing the intimate and unique experience.

Another intriguing aspect of the Tenement Museum is the meticulous attention to detail in the renovated apartments. You'll observe as you travel through these rooms that every aspect, the kitchen's utensils as well as the flooring, has been meticulously examined to give a real glimpse into the past. Festive motifs highlighting the numerous ways immigrant families cherished Christmas give a festive touch to these details throughout the holiday. Each of the modest trinkets, often handcrafted and inherited from earlier generations, has a special story about creativity and tradition. In addition to apartment visits, the Tenement Museum offers walking tours of the Lower East

Side, allowing visitors to see the neighborhood that was once home to waves of immigrants from all over the globe. These excursions draw attention to the stores, houses of worship, and public spaces that were significant to the immigrant experience, giving a richer backdrop for the stories told within the museum. These walking tours can include stops during the holidays that showcase regional celebrations, like the bustling marketplaces where families purchased holiday dinners and the places of worship where worshippers congregate to observe religious rituals.

The intricate and multifaceted experience provided by the strolling tours blends the individual stories of particular families with the broader social and cultural context of the neighborhood. With daily hours commencing at 10 AM, it's simple to fit a visit to the Tenement Museum into your itinerary. The $33 per person admission price includes a guided tour, and it is a quite reasonable rate for such an enjoyable and educational experience. Purchasing your tickets online in advance is important, more so if you have a particular tour in mind. For visitors who want to take a little piece of New York City home with them, the museum gift shop is a veritable gold mine of books, toys, and souvenirs. It's the perfect spot to find and secure a sentimental travel memory.

- **Museum at Eldridge Street**

The Museum at Eldridge Street, located at **12 Eldridge St., New York, NY 10002**, is a fascinating place with the combination of excellent architecture, cultural preservation, and a rich past. It is set in the renowned Eldridge Street Synagogue and provides visitors with a comprehensive glimpse into the lives of Eastern European Jewish immigrants who once called this region home.

Built in 1887 by Jewish exiles from Eastern Europe, the Eldridge Street Synagogue was the first large synagogue in the United States. Its remarkable design, influenced by Gothic, Romanesque, and Moorish styles, has ornate stained glass windows, ornate fixtures, and a beautiful sanctuary that has been painstakingly restored to its former splendor. The edifice, which was on the verge of being lost to neglect, is now a museum and a National Historic Landmark after a 20-year, $20 million restoration project. Guided tours bring the synagogue's history to life. These tours present an interesting window into the lives of Jewish refugees in the late 19th and early 20th centuries, examining how they maintained their customs while adapting to life in a new nation. The knowledgeable guides tell stories about the individuals who constructed the synagogue and the challenges they encountered as they show visitors throughout the beautifully restored building.

A holiday visit to the museum gives a unique perspective on how Jewish immigrants maintained their traditions among New York City's larger Christmas parties. The backdrop of the Christmas season reveals how several cultures prospered and coexisted in a heterogeneous city, despite the museum's primary emphasis on Jewish history. In addition to its remarkable physical style, the museum features a variety of exhibitions that delve into various aspects of Lower East Side Jewish culture. Often displayed here are menorahs, prayer books, and other sacred objects from the synagogue's historical past. These artifacts contribute to the narrative of the community's historical religious beliefs and practices. Plus, the museum offers special events, including lectures, workshops, and music that celebrate Jewish heritage. These programs give visitors additional chances to interact with the museum's exhibits and experience the synagogue's broader historical and cultural context. One of the best examples of the significant transformations that have taken place in New York throughout time is the Museum at Eldridge Street, situated in what is now Chinatown.

This offers visitors a different perspective on the area, allowing them to compare and contrast the historical Jewish residents of this area with the vibrant, diverse neighborhood it is now. The museum is open from 10 AM to 5 PM, and admission costs from $8 per person, making visiting an intriguing and reasonably priced experience. The museum is closed on certain days due to Saturdays being observed as the Jewish Sabbath, so make sure you schedule your visit appropriately.

EXPERIENCING THE HOLIDAY SPIRIT

What to Do and Where to Go on Christmas Eve and Day

New York during Christmas brings with it a wonderful experience, as the city transforms into a jovial winter wonderland. Christmas Eve and Day in NYC provide a variety of sites and activities that allow you to immerse yourself in the holiday spirit.

❖ **Attending midnight mass.**

For a midnight service, Christmas Eve is one of the best times to visit a church or one of the city's stunning landmarks. These ceremonies are not only very spiritual but also offer an opportunity to participate in a significant rite and appreciate the architectural splendor of New York's religious structure. A few churches also hold excellent choir performances to further enhance the experience and these places occasionally have midnight mass on Christmas Eve:

- **Cathedral Church of St. John the Divine**

Situated on Manhattan's Upper West Side at **1047 Amsterdam Ave., New York, NY 10025**, the Cathedral Church of St. John the Divine is a notable example of Gothic Revival architecture and a significant player in the social and religious life of New York City. It is the largest church in the world and a stunning place that combines religion, art, and history. Inside, the cathedral's enormous size and breathtaking architectural architecture astound visitors with its beautiful stained glass windows, elaborate stone sculptures, and towering ceilings that all combine to create an aura of awe.

Exploring every inch of the enormous and intricate edifice can take hours. One of the cathedral's primary characteristics is its magnificent pipe organ. An extraordinary acoustic experience, the 8,500-pipe organ produces a massive, powerful sound that reverberates across the large space. One of the cathedral's primary events is its superb organ, with a focal point for concerts and services. St. John the Divine has a very moving Christmas celebration. The Christmas Eve midnight mass at the cathedral draws attendees from all across the city, and it's a really poignant ceremony. A serene and contemplative atmosphere that captures the essence of the season is created by the exquisite surroundings, the exquisite ceremony, and the poignant organ music. Not only during the holidays, but all year round, St. John the Divine is a vibrant center of culture.

The church hosts several events, one of which is the well-known blessing of the animals, commemorating the Feast of St. Francis. Another amazing celebration features antique silent movies to complement live organ music. The cathedral is a vibrant and fascinating part of New York's cultural landscape because of these events, as well as the many art projects and exhibitions that it hosts. Visitors should also not miss exploring the grounds of the church. Its sense of wonder and serenity is enhanced by a magnificent sculpture in the grounds that depicts the creation of the cosmos. Plus, peacocks call the location home, adding to the unique and endearing experience. For guests interested in seeing more, the rooftop stroll offers breathtaking views of Central Park and the New York City skyline, giving a different perspective of the city. This tour is a terrific opportunity to acquire a new picture of the cathedral and grasp its significance in the city. For $15, adults can enter St. John the Divine, and inside, guests can focus on the church to maximize its benefits. along the aisles, observe the surroundings, and attempt to make it into a service or function.

- **St. Francis of Assisi Roman Catholic Church**

Love, religion, and community come together to form a particular experience in St. Francis of Assisi Roman Catholic Church, located at **135 W 31st St., New York, NY 10001**. This is especially true during Christmas as the chapel is well-known for its uncomplicated and hospitable atmosphere, offering a peaceful respite from the bustling city and making it a popular destination. The chapel exudes calm, beauty, and love with its amazing stained glass windows, intricate statuary, and a stunning altar that begs for reverence and introspection. The inside of the church is decked up with joyous

 decorations that symbolize the joy and optimism of the season, enhancing the already serene ambiance that permeates the place throughout the holidays. One moving event of the year is the midnight mass on Christmas Eve at St. Francis of Assisi. The intimate, serene environment and strong feeling of community that characterize the midnight mass make it a special occasion.

The audience is frequently moved to tears by the choir's performance that heightens the gravity and beauty of the event. Its beauty is almost Broadway-esque. The powerful message that is conveyed throughout the Mass tells everyone how important it is to concentrate on the true meaning of Christmas. Adding to being a house of worship, St. Francis of Assisi Church is a community that actively embodies the values of the saint bearing its name. The church's humanitarian initiatives, such as providing hot meals for the homeless, demonstrate its dedication to serving others. The church's dedication to generosity and equality forms the core of its mission. The pastor and church staff provide a warm welcome to all, irrespective of their ethnicity, origin, or life challenges. This spirit of openness and acceptance is eloquently captured in the church's Christmas sign, which reimagines Mary and Joseph as contemporary couples exploring the streets of New York City. It also serves as a powerful reminder of how universal their narrative is. The church is a convenient place, a flexible schedule for daily Mass, and a pleasant community.

It is easy for visitors to find a little peace in the center of the bustling metropolis because both the upper and lower churches have serene spaces for prayer and meditation at any time of day. The Shrine of St. Francis, located in the lower church, is a particularly beautiful and serene site of prayer with its unique charm and historical significance. Along with its spiritual qualities, St. Francis of Assisi is a place where art and history collide. The cathedral houses remnants of the World Trade Center and other magnificent artwork, and they serve as a poignant reminder of the city's resiliency and the enduring power of faith. Electric lights are accessible throughout the church so that guests can publicly offer their prayers, contributing to the overall atmosphere of reverence and tranquility that characterizes this sacred space.

- **Basilica of St. Patrick's Old Cathedral**

Located at **263 Mulberry St., New York, NY 10012**, the Basilica of St. Patrick's Old Cathedral is a historic Roman Catholic cathedral that has been an important part of the city since the early 1800s. This cathedral, a famous landmark renowned for its exquisite structure and lengthy history, was formerly the seat of the Archdiocese of New York. The church invites visitors to learn about its spiritual and cultural history every day starting at 9 a.m. Experience the warmth and festive spirit of Christmas in the Basilica of St. Patrick's Old Cathedral. The midnight service on Christmas Eve brings Christians from all over to celebrate in a welcoming and spiritual environment. Attending the evening Mass at 7 p.m., when the spirit of the season is quite evident, is an unforgettable experience. The church's organ and choir add magnificent music to the Mass, filling the air with reverence and awe as they play well-known songs like "Joy to the World" and "O Holy Night." The young priests educate the audience on crucial subjects with their insightful homilies. The presence of young people from the neighborhood really dedicated to their prayers adds vibrancy and happiness to the service. The church seems like a pleasant sanctuary in the heart of the bustling metropolis due to its sense of community and inclusivity.

The basilica's architecture is truly remarkable, with its elaborate stained glass windows, exquisite altar, and striking cross that towers above the main altar. The current renovations have enhanced its attractiveness even more, enabling visitors to appreciate the church's spiritual and historical significance. The church is filled with the heavenly beauty of the choir's voices and the thunderous tones of the organ during services. In addition to the Mass, history aficionados shouldn't miss the fascinating subterranean tour of the basilica. This

60- to 90-minute tour, which includes a visit to the subterranean cemetery and an explanation of the lives of notable Catholics who have influenced the church's legacy, offers an engrossing insight into the cathedral's past. The guide vividly brings history to life by narrating tales of the early refugees, their struggles, and their unwavering faith. Often referred to as the "pope's cathedral," the tunnels provide visitors with a profound and somber experience that serves as a reminder of the boundless life that awaits the pious. The trip's intellectual worth is enhanced by its well-paced schedule, with opportunities for introspection and prayer. The anecdotes along the journey are reminiscent of historical dramas like "Gangs of New York" and give depth and perspective, enhancing the trip's memory.

- **Church of St. Ignatius Loyola**

One of the most exquisite Catholic churches in New York City is the Church of St. Ignatius Loyola, located on Manhattan's Upper East Side at **980 Park Ave., New York, NY 10028**. This late 19th-century marvel, known for its exquisite marble work, ornate vaulted hall, and breathtaking stained glass windows, is a testament to both beauty and faith. Every day from 8:30 AM to 9:00 PM, it invites individuals from all walks of life to enjoy its serene environment and strong religious beliefs. Christmas at St. Ignatius Loyola is a particularly moving time that combines the ancient Catholic traditions with the breathtaking grandeur of the building. The Christmas Mass also unites Christians in celebration in an elegant but welcoming environment.

The Mass is opened and closed by exquisitely choreographed processions that are both solemn and elegant, establishing the mood for an enjoyable and deeply spiritual event. The gentle priests' teachings inspire hope and reflection in the audience, and these lessons stick with them long after the ceremony is over. The church's well-known music really comes to life during Christmas. An almost heavenly atmosphere is created by the powerful performance of the choir and the soaring tone of the organ. The powerful sound of the organ combined with the choir's vocals creates an atmosphere that raises the spirit and touches the heart. It's a touching experience to witness a St. Ignatius Loyola Christmas performance. The combination of the church's magnificent edifice, the excellent singing, and the well-curated program leaves a lasting effect on everyone who attends. Seeing the church by itself is breathtaking. Stepping inside unveils a world of intricate architectural details, luxurious marble, and very tall ceilings. Venetian artisans created the enormous marble statues that depict the Stations of the Cross, adding to the church's splendor.

The exquisitely crafted baptism font is a work of beauty in and of itself, seamlessly harmonizing with the church's design. St. Ignatius Loyola has a warm, inviting atmosphere that extends beyond its outward appeal. There are several Sunday Masses held in the church, each with a distinct goal. The magnificent church is used for a more conventional Mass, with the lovely sounds of the organ and choir filling the air. For families with young children, the basement mass is held in a less formal setting. This space is designed to accommodate small children who may need to move about or play around during the ceremony. Following Mass, parishioners can socialize over coffee, cookies, and discussion in the basement, which helps to deepen their sense of community.

Taking in the city's festive lights

For something less formal, see for yourself the city's Christmas lights while strolling about. The streets of Manhattan are ablaze with Christmas lights, showcasing striking stores and whole skyscrapers decorated in festive colors. A traditional NYC Christmas experience involves enjoying hot chocolate while taking a leisurely stroll through these illuminated streets.

On Christmas Eve, enjoy seasonal cocktails at one of the city's pop-ups or small bars with a seasonal theme. These places are decked out for the holidays and have a warm atmosphere perfect for unwinding with eggnog, mulled wine, or hot cider as it is a wonderful way to unwind and feel festive. Here is a short descriptive list of New York's pop-ups and tiny bars that feature seasonal themes and are perfect for a fun drink on Christmas Eve:

- **Miracle on 9th Street**

Miracle on 9th Street is a pop-up cocktail bar with a Christmas theme and miraculously brings the joy of the season to life. Nestled in the East Village at **649**

E 9th St., New York, NY 10009, this small and vibrant neighborhood is a winter paradise, with a celebratory vibe that permeates every square inch. The décor is charmingly tacky, with an explosion of ornaments, tinsel, and glittering lights that hang from the ceiling to the floor.

You get the feeling that you've walked into the most exciting company Christmas party you've ever been to, thanks to the warm and inviting atmosphere. The bar is well recognized for its creative holiday drinks, all of which are presented in festive glasses that often double as keepsakes. Strong and delicious, "Jingle Ball Nog"-style cocktails give a bit of Christmas flavor with every sip. The staff is as happy as Santa himself, and everyone who passes through the door is instantly swept up in the Christmas mood thanks to their festive apparel. Drinks at Miracle on 9th Street are reasonably priced, with items costing between $20 and $30. They are delicious and festive and each drink has been thoughtfully created to evoke the spirit of Christmas, with tastes that evoke recollections of holiday food and traditions. The revenues from the sale of the bar's collector mugs are also donated to SEVA, an organization that gives eye care to individuals in need. To avoid the crowds and ensure a spot at the bar, where the cozy, joyous ambiance is most appreciated, it's a good idea to arrive early. Friendly and courteous, the bartenders often help customers choose the perfect holiday drink from the menu.

- **Gallow Green**

Gallow Green is a delightful rooftop restaurant and bar located above the McKittrick Hotel at **542 W 27th St., New York, NY 10001**; a quirky oasis in the heart of the city. This year-round green space is particularly beautiful in the winter, when Christmas décor and glittering lights turn it into a snowy wonderland. There is an abundance of lush foliage that exudes the tranquility of a garden, making the ambiance cozy and welcoming. The bar area is charmingly adorned for Christmas, making it a fantastic spot for a holiday lunch or seasonal drink.

It has a sophisticated and relaxed vibe. The yurt

 seating adds a unique, intimate touch to the rooftop, allowing visitors to spend the evening in a luxurious, inviting, semi-private space. The employees at Gallow Green give exceptional customer service and ensure a fantastic holiday evening. The cuisine at Gallow Green is as impressive as the restaurant's atmosphere. The menu has meals that range in price from $30 to $50, all of which are professionally prepared and blend satisfying and refined tastes.

Because of its huge, succulent shrimp, the shrimp cocktail stands out as having the ideal combination of taste and freshness. Another delight is the Gallow Green salad that astounds visitors with a harmonious fusion of tastes that elevates a straightforward meal to extraordinary heights. The menu's highlights are the imaginatively designed cocktails, like the "Garden Shed," which blends gin with an infusion of cucumber and red bell pepper.

- **Oscar Wilde**

Oscar Wilde is a Victorian-style restaurant that expertly blends the refinement of the past with the vitality of the contemporary situated at **45 W 27th St., New York, NY 10001.** This gastropub is a visual feast with its elaborate design and antique décor, offering a unique blend of historical charm and modern flare. Oscar Wilde is transformed into a festive paradise for the holidays, along with some of the most gorgeous and elaborate décor one could imagine.

An exciting environment is created when the refined feel of an old-fashioned tavern combines with the celebratory mood of the holidays and a lengthy marble bar with a wide selection of over 300 whiskey kinds, innovative drinks, and delicious American meals that complement the ambiance serving as the space's focal point. Oscar Wilde assures that all visitors will have an amazing and unique experience in an exquisite environment. It's the ideal spot for escaping into a timeless realm of beauty over the holidays because of the ambiance that perfectly combines Victorian grandeur with Christmas happiness. The menu at Oscar Wilde is similarly impressive, with the same painstaking attention to detail seen in the architectural design. The menu features a selection of American appetizers that are all masterfully prepared to elevate ordinary pub cuisine to new levels. Try the thick, velvety sauce of the truffle gnocchi if you're yearning for comfort cuisine with a gourmet twist. The steak sandwich, sliders, and burger are popular selections; these substantial, full foods go nicely with a large assortment of beverages.

The drinks at Oscar Wilde are amazing, offering a wide selection to satisfy any palate. All of the cocktails are well crafted, including the inventive creations with an Alice in Wonderland theme and the more conventional options like the old-fashioned. The bar serves a particularly delicious passion fruit drink, also topped with white chocolate and has a nice combination of sweetness and tanginess.

- **Mace**

Located at **35 W 8th St., New York, NY 10011**,
 Mace is a tiny and mighty cocktail bar that has made a name for itself as a destination for foodies and cocktail enthusiasts seeking out exceptional fare. Renowned French bartender Nico de Soto and Cocktail Kingdom's Greg Boehm made sure Mace launched in 2015 and was named one of the World's 50 Best Bars for three years in a row. The bar's name alludes to its dedication to using unique spices that are found globally, transforming each drink into a multisensory experience.

The space itself is cozy, with brick walls, banquette seats, and stools that give a hint of rustic elegance. The holidays add a seasonal charm to Mace's already wonderful environment, making it the ideal spot to warm up with a unique craft drink among the festive merriment. The inventive and surprising ways that spices can lift a drink's taste are shown on Mace's cocktail menu, which is a credit to the mixologists' talent. Each drink is a brilliant masterpiece, with ingredients like the earthy richness of black truffle, the fragrant appeal of rosemary, and the nutty nuances of sesame. The bar's food offerings are a delightful surprise for visitors only anticipating beverages, thanks to its menu.

Christmas Morning Brunch

Start your Christmas Day with a memorable breakfast at one of the most well-known eats in New York. Numerous places offer holiday-themed typical American cuisine and fancier selections like lobster breakfast or dinners with truffle taste. Bookings are often required, so be sure to reserve your spot in advance to guarantee it.

- **Russ & Daughters Cafe**

 Nestled at **127 Orchard St., New York, NY 10002**, Russ & Daughters Cafe is a well-known establishment that offers a cozy refuge of comforting Jewish cuisine. The café, opened in 2014 to honor the 100th anniversary of the well-known Russ & Daughters candy, perfectly encapsulates the vibrant culture of the Lower East Side. Stepping into this retro-themed restaurant is like stepping into a big family, where both new and regulars are welcomed with equal affection. The homey feel of the

establishment makes it the ideal place for a delectable, sentimental Christmas brunch. The café gives a setting that is both vibrant and historic, particularly in the winter when the atmosphere is filled with the spirit of the season. Its traditional appeal is mirrored in its décor, ageless and dating back to a century. Every item on the Russ & Daughters Cafe menu has been thoughtfully prepared to both pay homage to the restaurant's historic Jewish background and to satisfy contemporary tastes. The meal is an ode to classic Jewish cooking. For $20 to $30 per item, diners can enjoy traditional meals like potato latkes, enriched with a luscious sprinkling of salmon roe, or bagel and lox that go wonderfully with their renowned cream cheese.

The café also offers inventive menu items, like fish cured with pastrami and served with velvety goat cheese. Those who appreciate a modern twist on a traditional meal will love this combo. Russ & Daughters Cafe is a one-of-a-kind experience that provides the perfect diversion from the winter cold. Every taste of the café's great cuisine and welcoming ambiance is full of flavor and history.

- **Clinton St. Baking Company**

The hidden culinary gem Clinton St. Baking Company is located at **4 Clinton St., New York, NY 10002**, and is especially amazing around the holidays. Since its establishment in 2001, the chef-owned American restaurant and bakery has been well-known for its renowned pancakes, substantial breakfasts, and brunches. The restaurant's commitment to quality is evident in every dish since its ingredients are acquired from reputable local vendors.

Every day starting at 9 AM, the Clinton St. Baking Company serves a large array of dishes, from breakfast through supper, including delectable desserts and classic American brunch cuisine. Plus, the takeaway section makes sure you can enjoy the holidays wherever you are. The culinary experience at Clinton St. Baking Company is nothing short of outstanding, and at $20 to $30 per dish, it's a terrific option for a festive and affordable

Christmas feast. The standout item on the menu is unquestionably the light and fluffy blueberry pancakes, mostly when coupled with the restaurant's unique maple butter that elevates the meal to a whole new level. The magic doesn't stop there. There are alternatives to suit every appetite, such as the brioche French toast and the substantial country breakfast. The ambience of Clinton St. Baking Company adds to its charm, setting a peaceful and comfortable counterpoint to the busy Christmas season. Because of its popularity, keep in mind that there are often waits, but the experience is definitely worth it. If you are fortunate enough to get a seat, the level of service is outstanding, making every guest feel appreciated and looked after.

- **Good Enough to Eat**

Good Enough to Eat, a well-liked Upper West Side staple since 1981, creates a joyful and cozy eating environment. The popular eatery is located at **520 Columbus Ave., New York, NY 10024**, and is well-known for its dedication to selling real American comfort cuisine that is prepared from scratch using the greatest local ingredients. Every dish at Good Enough to Eat showcases the restaurant's persistent commitment to excellence.

 It's a cozy, friendly space with a lively vibe that embodies the spirit of the holidays. This restaurant is perfect for a quick bite to eat after visiting nearby sites like the Natural History Museum or for a leisurely holiday dinner. On weekdays, it opens at 8 AM, while on weekends, it opens at 9 AM. Good Enough to Eat offers a wonderful menu with meals ranging from $20 to $30, making it an affordable and enjoyable choice for holiday eating.

Because of their tasty and light texture, the blueberry pancakes with strawberry butter are one of the most popular alternatives, and they have a dedicated fan following. When it comes to savory dishes, the poached eggs with house-made corned beef are a highlight. It emphasizes the restaurant's dedication to making all of its soups, sauces, freshly baked bread, and desserts.

- **Cafe Mogador**

Cafe Mogador, tucked at **101 St. Marks Pl., New**

York, NY 10009, has been a popular destination for visitors since 1983 who want to savor the aromatic and tasty food of Morocco and the Middle East. This family-run restaurant is particularly lovely around Christmas, when its cozy atmosphere sets the perfect refuge from the winter chill. Holiday brunch or a celebratory supper are ideal at Cafe Mogador, which is open from 10 AM on weekdays and 9:30 AM on weekends.

Its extensive menu offers both filling and healthy choices. The restaurant is spacious and intimate, with a huge, bohemian air that draws in a wide and lively audience. The aroma of freshly prepared meals and the sound of animated conversations create a constant, vibrant atmosphere. The majority of the classic Moroccan meals on Cafe Mogador's menu are priced between $20 and $30, so you can have a filling and delicious supper without going over your budget. Sample some of their specialties, like the tagine because of its flawlessly cooked meats and vegetables and provides a flavor of authentic Moroccan comfort cuisine. With its fresh pita and creamy hummus, the Middle Eastern platter is another classic that's perfect for sharing. The meal's rich, spicy tastes pair beautifully with the refreshing taste of the mint lemonade. Numerous vegetarian and gluten-free choices are offered to accommodate a range of dietary requirements.

- **Friedman's**

Friedman's at **50 W 72nd St., New York, NY 10023**, is a lovely escape from the hustle and bustle of New York. It has a warm, woodsy environment that feels particularly homey around Christmas. Known for its commitment to casual American comfort food, this laid-back restaurant has made a name for itself as a pioneer in the gluten-free eating industry. Friedman's, open every day from 9 AM to 9 PM, provides a friendly setting in which diners get to experience refined variations on classic deli and diner food, complemented by the enticement of outdoor sitting. The background music, often jazz-infused, creates a relaxed and sophisticated atmosphere. Friedman's is a satisfying and affordable alternative because of its delicious and wide menu, most of which are priced between $20 and $30. The savory joys of a gluten-free burger and the incredibly light and fluffy berry compote brioche French toast provide something for everyone.

The Korean wings, known for their incredible size and deep taste, are a must-try, and the yuca fries give a delightful side that pairs well with many of the meals. For enjoying a heartier meal that tastes exactly like home, the club sandwich, tuna melt, and grilled cheese are all fantastic choices. The cocktail menu is excellent, too; options like the French 75 give a subtle and powerful counterpoint to the food.

- **Jack's Wife Freda**

Jack's Wife Freda, situated at **226 Lafayette St., New York, NY 10012,** is a cheerful and inviting restaurant with a remarkable combination of

American and Mediterranean cuisine, perfect for the holidays. Open every day from 8:30 AM, this  popular New York City café has a reputation for creating a welcoming atmosphere and treating every customer like family. With its clean, modest decor and outside seating that provides a wonderful roadside dining experience, the space is reminiscent of a charming Parisian café.

Inside, the atmosphere is just as warm, offering a stylish and comfortable refuge from the hustle and bustle of the holidays. The cuisine is visually arresting as well as excellent, and emphasizes colorful, fresh ingredients that still perfectly capture Mediterranean tastes while being prepared in a very American way. Most of the offerings on Jack's Wife Freda's adaptable, 24-hour menu are priced between $20 and $30. Specialty meals give a gentler, lighter take on the traditional Mediterranean staple. One such dish is the Green Shakshuka, having precisely cooked eggs and a green sauce that pairs beautifully with freshly baked bread. For a heartier fare, the special breakfast, consisting of lamb, red potatoes, and avocado and topped with a poached egg, is a must-taste dish. The waffles, which are a customer favorite, have syrup, mixed berries, and whipped cream on them, giving a sweet counterpoint to the savory entrees. The café also has an amazing selection of classic drinks that go nicely with the tasty and seasonal cuisine.

Enjoying the rest of the Festive Day

Think about spending your morning taking a leisurely stroll in Central Park. The park is serene on Christmas Day, offering a serene diversion from the city's regular hustle and bustle. You will appreciate the beauty of the most well-known green space in New York while taking in the views of the snow-covered surroundings, the chilly winter air, and perhaps even some ice dancers at Wollman Rink. Many of the larger markets would be closed on Christmas Day, but a few smaller ones would be open, giving shoppers a last-minute opportunity to pick up unique gifts or goodies. The festive atmosphere, twinkling lights, and aroma of delectable cuisine make these markets a delight to visit on Christmas Day.

While you're making your schedule, consider these additional enjoyable activities. You can choose a place from the ones we've listed that suits your interests:

- New York ice skating is a traditional winter pastime. It's an encounter that perfectly captures the essence of the season. These rinks are delightful to see and beautifully designed, even if you are not a skater.

- The city is filled with themed restaurants and pop-up bars that go all out for the holidays. You can enjoy festive beverages while immersing yourself in an immersive Christmas experience that is decorated with lights, ornaments, and other decorations.

- Apart from the famous exhibits in Manhattan, remarkable decorations can be seen in many other communities around the city. Take a walk around these neighborhoods on Christmas Eve or Christmas Day to experience the spirit of the season without the crowds.

- Several museums in NYC include holiday-themed displays and activities if you'd like a more sedate Christmas. It's a fantastic way to take in the city's cultural offerings while staying warm.

Attending a Holiday Performance

One of the finest ways to experience the enchantment and wonder of the season is to attend a Christmas performance. The most well-known is the Radio City Christmas Spectacular with the Rockettes. Visitors have been enthralled with this incredible spectacle at Radio City Music Hall since 1933, as previously explained. It has timeless Christmas music, stunning special effects, and exquisite choreography. Much thought has gone into ensuring that every aspect of the performance fosters a welcoming environment that appeals to both residents and visitors. It unites people, evoking sentiments of nostalgia and happiness long after the final curtain rises.

While reflecting the spirit of the season, these concerts provide a warm and often more intimate experience and if you want to watch a holiday play in New York over Christmas, here are a few more spots that won't break the bank:

- **Theater for the New City**

Theater for the New City is a great venue to witness

experimental and socially aware productions. The off-Broadway theatrical scene centers around **155 1st Ave., New York, NY 10003**. Founded in 1970, this non-profit organization presents 30 to 40 plays annually. For aspiring performers and writers, it's a crucial platform for getting their work heard. Its mission is to stretch the boundaries of traditional theater by presenting a diverse range of tales that question, inspire, and provoke.

Because of its strong community links and commitment to originality, the theater gives a vital platform for new voices in American theater. During the holidays, Theater for the New City becomes a center for holiday-themed creativity, showcasing shows that blend comedy, social criticism, and poignant storytelling. Unlike traditional Christmas shows, these performances can leave spectators emotionally engaged and amazed. The White Blacks is one particularly notable show that exemplifies how theater addresses challenging issues. The drama explores the identification problems faced by a Black Creole family in a society where white racial values are the norm. It's a must-see over the holidays because of its outstanding acting, clever comedy, and immersive stage design that immerses the audience in the characters' world. For its holiday programming, Theater for the New City has also embraced virtual and outdoor events, so even in tough times, its creative goal will continue. The Open 'tho Shut' Revue, a prominent element of the neighborhood's holiday festivities, includes live acts every Saturday in the 'Garage' Theater on East 10th Street.

And here is where viewers can join in on the joyous atmosphere of this open-air extravaganza. One example of the theater's virtual programming that shows its dedication to preserving access to the arts is the Lower East Side Festival of the Arts, an annual event that has successfully moved online and increased its reach. Theater for the New City extends its holiday programming by presenting street theater works that go directly to city neighborhoods, engaging the community all year long. The theater's commitment to utilizing the arts to bring about good change is seen in the frequency with which these free performances tackle social justice and concerns of community empowerment. Plus, the theater hosts seminars and readings that give a stage for budding artists to develop and showcase their work. Because of its friendly environment, Theater for the New City is a vital resource for New York's creative community.

- **The Players Theatre**

 The Players Theatre is a mainstay of New York City's theatrical industry, beloved for its small-scale productions and extensive history. This well-established theater, situated at **115 MacDougal St., New York, NY 10012**, is a cultural icon that has been entertaining audiences for almost fifty years. The Players Theatre presents a unique blend of artistic and historical experiences; its main stage features a wide variety of plays, its rehearsal halls are buzzing with creative energy, and the legendary Café Wha? is just around the corner. The theater's friendly, welcoming atmosphere and excellent plays make it

a well-liked hangout for people of all ages. For Christmas, the Players Theatre becomes a whimsical paradise that draws families and theatergoers alike with its charming seasonal plays. One of the highlights of the season is the annual performance of "A Christmas Carol," a timeless classic that has established itself as a staple of the theater's holiday repertoire. This play is a wonderful celebration of the season, with a talented cast and crew from Literally Alive bringing the magic of Christmas to life with each performance.

The musical and visual elements of the production are masterfully crafted to transport audiences to Victorian England and immerse them in the world of Ebenezer Scrooge and his ghostly visitors. Although the theater is rather tiny, the performances are excellent, with a cast that plays their roles with passion and accuracy, as well as music that is perfectly synchronized to the events taking place on stage. Actors and crew often engage the audience in a question-and-answer session after concerts, particularly around the holidays, providing an intimate glimpse into the creative process. The intimate touch that this engagement brings will make the event more memorable for families and younger people. The theater itself, however tiny and intimate, enhances the watching experience by creating a tight connection between the audience and the artists. The rather small seats are more than made up for by the theater's setting that is full of antique charm and historic appeal. Adding to the Christmas Carol, the Players Theatre hosts many other productions all year long, including works by well-known authors like Agatha Christie. And whether they are seasonal classics or year-round plays, fans appreciate the theater's commitment to providing engaging, high-quality performances and continually enjoy these shows.

- **Queens Theatre**

Situated at **14 United Nations Ave S, Flushing Meadows Corona Park, Queens, NY 11368**, Queens Theatre is a bustling cultural hub that perfectly captures the richness of Queens, the nation's most ethnically diverse county. Originating in the 1964 World's Fair, the theater has grown into one of the main venues for the performing arts, presenting a diverse range of acts to cater to the

2.2 million residents of Queens and the surrounding regions. In order to benefit the community, the theater presents plays that are of a high standard, diverse, and accessible. Its three distinct performance spaces are the 472-seat Claire Shulman Theatre, the 99-seat Studio Theatre, and the intimate 70-seat Cabaret. The theater can accommodate a wide range of events, including large-scale shows and intimate performances, since each chamber has its own appeal.

The glass-walled Nebula Lobby that welcomes visitors with a cozy ambiance, adds a modern touch. The Queens Theatre's holiday shows bring the theater to life and captivate audiences of all ages. One of the highlights of the season is the annual production of "A Christmas Carol" by the Titan Theatre Company. This production is well known for its outstanding performers, vibrant costumes, and simple and impactful staging. It's the perfect way to get into the Christmas mood, with a timeless message and a compelling performance. Aside from that, the theater hosts other holiday shows. A notable performance is "Navidad" by the Calpulli Mexican Dance Company that pays homage to Mexican Christmas traditions with vibrant dance and music. For seeking something new, this show is a must-see as it adds a unique cultural flair to the festive season. Plus, there are kid-friendly theatrical shows meant to entertain younger audiences as well as adults, making them the perfect family activity.

The theater's commitment to inclusion and education is evident in these plays, since they often include interactive aspects that encourage children to engage in the storyline. The theater's setting adds to its allure. The site, set in a park with the iconic Unisphere and the "flying saucers" from "Men in Black," provides a beautiful and interesting background. Apart from its annual theatrical plays, Queens Theatre hosts an array of cultural activities all year long. These include participatory musical events for kids and concerts featuring local and international performers, such as Indian classical dance. The venue is flexible for the community because it can also accommodate private gatherings.

FESTIVE HIDDEN GEMS AND OFF-THE-BEATEN PATH EXPERIENCES

Exploring NYC's Lesser-Known Festive Spots

New York is well-known for its stunning holiday lights and famous Christmas customs, but some of its most lovely holiday experiences are tucked away from the usual tourist trails. You will get a more intimate and affordable taste of the city's festive mood by visiting these lesser-known Christmas locations. The Rockefeller Center Christmas tree and the Fifth Avenue window displays attract large crowds, but NYC has many additional holiday jewels with a more personal, local experience. These places are perfect for having a festive and quiet exploration of the city.

Explore the areas where New Yorkers themselves celebrate the holidays to get started. Although Dyker Heights in Brooklyn is well-known for its extravagant Christmas light displays, nearby Bay Ridge also boasts beautiful displays without the same volume of visitors. You are welcome to wander slowly around these areas and spend some time taking in the decorations and lights.

- **Museum of the Moving Image**

Nestled at **36-01 35th Ave, Queens, NY 11106**, the Museum of the Moving Image (MoMI) is a real treasure mine for aficionados of films, TV series, and digital media. This museum presents a captivating Christmas experience and is the only one in the United States dedicated to examining the creative processes behind these forms of entertainment.

With admission prices starting from $22, it's an affordable and worthwhile experience for families, couples and solo travelers. "Behind the Screen," MoMI's major feature, explains to visitors the intricate process of making, advertising, and exhibiting movies and television series in a dynamic environment. A must-see during Christmas is a multimedia experience that brings the enchantment of the screen to life, replete with sound design stations and antique cameras. Christmas at MoMI is a special time of year, full of holiday activities and seasonal films. One of the best vacation attractions is "The Jim Henson Exhibition." In celebration of Jim Henson's creativity, see original artwork, antique puppets, and never-before-seen footage from beloved shows like Sesame Street and The Muppet Show. While this show is captivating on its own, the holidays heighten its allure.

Because MoMI's interactive exhibitions allow visitors to engage directly with the material, families are particularly attracted. Make your flip book and try voiceovers and sound effects. These activities are both entertaining and give a deeper understanding of the motion picture's history. The MoMI's impressive collection of vintage cameras provides an overview of the advancements in filmmaking technology. This exhibit is particularly charming during Christmas since it brings back memories of classic films that have become seasonal favorites. Warm and welcoming, the Museum of the Moving Image is a wonderful spot to spend a winter's day, and it's easily accessible from Manhattan by train.

- **Merchant's House Museum**

Located at **29 E 4th St., New York, NY 10003**, the Merchant's House Museum gives a unique perspective into the history of New York during the 19th century, making it a perfect destination for a holiday visit. With entrance fees beginning at $20 per person, this historic mansion sets an immersive experience that transports you to a period when the city was still blossoming.

The Merchant's House was built in 1832 and purchased by wealthy hardware merchant Seabury Tredwell in 1835. Constructed in the Federal and Greek Revival styles, this row house was inhabited for over a century by the Tredwell family and is now among the most well-preserved examples of its type in the city. Visitors get to tour four levels of period rooms filled with the family's original furniture, antiquities, books, and even clothing to get a close-up look at an affluent family's lifestyle in mid-19th century New York. The museum comes to life around the holidays, the home is decorated in a Victorian manner, evoking nostalgia for earlier Christmas traditions. As you walk through the front door, the scent of pine and the warm glow of candles set the scene for a nostalgic journey. The museum's carefully curated collection of holiday décor that includes wreaths, garlands, and an exquisitely decorated Christmas tree, aims to evoke the customs and tastes of the Tredwell family while also fostering a true festive feel.

One of the best things about visiting the Merchant's House during Christmas are the holiday-themed tours and festivities. The Tredwell family's Christmas celebration is explored in full, down to the food and presents they would have given, during special guided tours offered by the museum. These tours bring the home to life with the assistance of informed interpreters who tell stories and anecdotes that vividly reflect 19th-century holiday customs. The museum is one of New York's most haunted mansions, and gives an additional layer of mystery for those interested in the paranormal. The ancient home is an interesting site with an ominous ambiance and rich history for a bit of a spooky thrill combined with Christmas happiness. In addition to the home itself, visitors can explore the museum's secret 19th-century garden. Even in the winter, this little and quaint neighborhood offers a peaceful diversion from the hustle and bustle of the metropolis. The meticulously tended plants in the historically inspired garden provide a serene environment for a walk or quiet period of reflection. The Merchant's House Museum is open Wednesday through Sunday from 12 p.m. to 5 p.m. and is conveniently located within a short walk of the 8th Street metro station.

- **Bronx Little Italy**

Bronx Little Italy, set at **2396 Arthur Ave., Bronx, NY 10458**, is a charming destination that promises a lovely experience, especially during the winter. This little area, known for its Italian roots, is a hidden treasure with a vintage charm and a festive vibe. Arthur Avenue is transformed into a dazzling winter paradise with festive décor and brilliant lights. You can sense the season's warmth and

liveliness as you stroll about. The neighborhood's

unique ambiance that stems from its Italian history, along with its welcoming nature, makes it an excellent choice for holiday gatherings. Prince Coffee House is a charming spot to start your vacation, renowned for its excellent coffee and cozy ambiance. It's the perfect place to toast to the season, enjoy a hot beverage, and people-watch. Next, go over to the Arthur Avenue Retail Market, which is a hub for some of the best Italian cuisine around. This indoor market offers a selection of fresh pasta, cheeses, sausages, and other items.

The market's lively ambiance and extensive assortment make it a must-visit, more so to carry some authentic Italian products home. The neighborhood's reputation is also attributed to its charming pastry shops and bakeries. The Artuso Bakery is also a must-see, with delicious Italian desserts like cannoli and tiramisu. The bakery's mouth watering pastries and lively décor will undoubtedly give your holiday party a pleasant touch. Bronx Little Italy is another vibrant area that recognizes its Albanian and Latino residents. This cross-cultural mingling gives a variety of dining options and improves the neighborhood's culinary scene. There's something to sate your appetite for Albanian, Italian, or Latin American food. Although more accessible to Manhattan than its tourist-heavy cousin, Bronx Little Italy provides a more authentic experience. Exploring the area is enjoyable because it has a real charm and a sense of community. The bakeries, eateries, and businesses in the area are ideal for the holidays and give a flavor of local customs and culture.

- **Washington Square Park**

Washington Square Park at **New York, NY 10012**, is a hidden gem and a little less busy. The park's grand arch, vibrant atmosphere, and excellent people-watching possibilities make it an excellent site to come over the holidays with a unique blend of city vitality and holiday charm. The park is open daily from 6 AM to 12 AM, and comes alive in the winter with a serene and vibrant ambiance. When the park's well-known Washington Arch is beautifully decorated for the holidays, it creates a striking background for pictures. With a spectacular

 Christmas tree close by, the festive mood is enhanced and a beautiful, almost mystical scene is created, particularly in the gentle glow of the evening lights. The park is humming with activity all year round as locals and tourists alike take advantage of its numerous attractions. The air is filled with music as talented street performers play celebratory melodies, creating a joyful ambiance across the region. It's a wonderful place to unwind and take in the sights and sounds, with people gathered from all walks of life to enjoy the season.

Despite the cold, Washington Square Park is bustling with visitors going about their daily lives. The park exudes warmth and camaraderie, families enjoying leisurely strolls and students from the adjacent NYU campus coming together with friends. The crowd's diversity is a reflection of the park's special status as a meeting point of cultures and experiences. One of the park's most beloved attractions is the center fountain that attracts tourists all year round. Winter or not, the fountain enhances the park's allure by acting as a hub for people to congregate and take in the joyous ambiance. There are seats everywhere, making it the perfect place to unwind, have a hot beverage, and soak in the joyous mood. The park is a popular destination for families on vacation because of its dog-friendly areas and kid-friendly play area, ensuring that everyone will have fun. Long-term park visits are also made more convenient by the availability of public bathrooms. While admiring the park's winter beauty, visitors can have a meal or snack from one of the numerous takeaway choices available at the nearby restaurants and food kiosks.

- **Morris-Jumel Mansion**

Located at **65 Jumel Terrace, New York, NY 10032**, high atop Mount Morris in the Washington Heights district, is the Morris-Jumel Mansion, Manhattan's oldest surviving residence. It's a place where history and the spirit of the holidays come together nicely. Built in 1765, this fabled home has seen hundreds of years of New York City's history, from its start during the American Revolution to its present role as a richly historical museum. The  home is open every day except Monday and offers visitors a rare glimpse into New York's rich history. Upon entering the mansion, one is transported back to the American Revolutionary War, when it served as General George Washington's headquarters. The mansion, steeped in history, has seen both American and British forces pass through its walls. Eliza Jumel, a well-known 19th-century lady who briefly wed former vice president Aaron Burr, later lived there.

When the Morris-Jumel Mansion is decorated with historically authentic pieces that evoke the elegance and charm of the early 19th century, it takes on a mysterious air during Christmas. The home is the perfect place for a holiday because of the joyful mood that the museum's seasonal performances and family-friendly activities generate. Experience how the holidays could have been enjoyed more than 200 years ago by traveling back in time to the historic grounds that include a peaceful lawn and garden that stand in stark contrast to the bustling metropolis outside. The mansion's well-preserved historical chambers are one of its key attractions. Seven of the nine rooms on show include scenes from the Jumel Era, illustrating the opulent lifestyle of the period. The octagonal dining room, furnished with exquisite detailing and with a glimpse into the lavish settings in which the Jumel family may have had holiday celebrations. As you explore the mansion, you will learn of the amazing tales that shaped its past. Eliza Jumel, the mansion's most well-known tenant, was an intriguing and fiercely ambitious lady.

Her marriage with Aaron Burr; famous for his fight with Alexander Hamilton further dramatizes the mansion's history. Even parts of the very famous musical Hamilton, composed by Lin Manuel-Miranda, were written in Burr's former chamber. During the holidays, the house gives visitors the chance to take advantage of a variety of cultural activities, such as art exhibitions and haunting tours that delve into the mansion's enigmatic history. The mansion's supposed ghost tours add mystery and excitement to a visit, particularly on the darker, colder winter days. The mansion's seasonal decorations and themed events create a warm, inviting atmosphere that's perfect for families and history enthusiasts looking for a more relaxed experience.

- **Brooklyn's Greenwood Cemetery**

Visitors will enjoy a peaceful and unique experience in Brooklyn's Greenwood Cemetery that blends history, art, and natural beauty. Not only is this treasured National Historic Landmark **(500 25th St., Brooklyn, NY 11232)** a 478-acre historic cemetery built in 1838, but it is also the last resting place of many famous persons. Originally used as a battlefield during the Revolution, the cemetery has been beautifully restored and now has ornate sculptures, monuments, and mausoleums.

It is the oldest surviving cemetery in Manhattan, with a rich historical tapestry reflecting the different cultural and historical traditions of New York City. Visitors are welcome to explore the expansive grounds of the cemetery, dotted with outstanding specimens of funerary art and architecture from many centuries. Around Christmas, Greenwood Cemetery has a certain beauty of its own. The cemetery's quiet winter landscape, with its snow-covered walks and tranquil atmosphere, offers a tranquil get-away from the bustling metropolis. Every day, starting at 7 a.m. The cemetery is open until 7pm, so visitors have lots of opportunities to enjoy its serene winter splendor. Though individual Christmas festivities may vary from year to year, the overall festive mood is apparent, with occasional holiday-themed excursions and activities that highlight the season's subtle elegance.

A paper map is given at the Prospect Park West gate so that visitors can explore the vast grounds. The map is a priceless resource since it provides information on well-known sites, notable historical figures, and significant architectural elements. There is an app for those who prefer digital materials, but when exploring the various routes inside the cemetery, it is best to use the printed map. Greenwood Cemetery is renowned for its breathtaking views and diverse natural environs. The two lakes, an abundance of greenery, and the well-maintained cemetery grounds come together to form a beautiful view that changes with the seasons. The peaceful ambiance of the cemetery is enhanced by the winter's light snowfall and cool air. Visitors can enjoy the striking contrasts between the intricate masonry of the monuments and the winter landscape by taking a leisurely walk along its paths. The cemetery holds a variety of cultural and educational activities all year long.

Walking tours through history are available, as well as talks and art exhibitions. During Christmas, special excursions that delve deeper into history highlight the cemetery's historical importance and its famous occupants. Plus, it's a beneficial idea to confirm in advance whether there will be any special events or seasonal changes to the operating hours.

- **Queens County Farm Museum**

Nestled at **73-50 Little Neck Pkwy, Queens, NY 11004**, the historic Queens County Farm Museum dates back to 1697, making it one of the state's oldest continuously farmed locations. This 47-acre

 treasure serves as both a tribute to New York's agricultural heritage and a vibrant center for education and community activity. Visit the Queens County Farm Museum to go back in time. It is open every day starting at 10 a.m. until 5:00 p.m. The farm has a beautifully renovated colonial home surrounded by fruit trees, vegetable gardens, and animal pens. This living museum showcases the growth of farming in New York City and places an emphasis on sustainable agricultural practices.

The farm offers guided tours and interactive displays that allow visitors to explore many aspects of the farm's history. These educational programs teach information on traditional agricultural practices and the farm's historical relevance in the area. The farm's diverse landscapes, including vegetable gardens and ancient buildings, present a glimpse into the city's agricultural history. During the holidays, the Queens County Farm Museum is turned into a joyful paradise. The Winter Lantern

Festival that showcases exquisitely carved lanterns that create a vivid rainbow of color throughout the farm, is a highlight of the season. These lanterns, with their representations of mythological creatures and festive themes, enchant visitors of all ages. Beyond the event, there are seasonal activities and marketplaces. Visitors can choose from a variety of foods served by local vendors, including tacos, dumplings, and hot chocolate. The farm also has a holiday market where guests can purchase Christmas trees, wreaths, and other seasonal decor. All ages are invited to visit the Queens County Farm Museum, since it is well-known for its engaging educational programs.

The farm also gives knowledgeable insights into New York City's agricultural history via guided tours of its historic buildings and grounds. These excursions normally feature exhibits of traditional agricultural techniques along with discussions about sustainable agriculture. The farm has engaging family-friendly events, such as hayrides, petting zoos, and seasonal activities. These initiatives aim to give a greater understanding of agricultural methods and environmental care. Apart from exploring the farm's grounds and learning about its history, guests can participate in interactive experiences that underscore the significance of local food networks. Apart from its informative and seasonal programs, the Queens County Farm Museum offers a tranquil escape from the fast-paced urban environment. Furthermore, because there is no entry fee, it is an affordable and easily accessible tourist site. Among the year-round special events hosted at the farm are seasonal festivals and educational activities. Keep in mind to check their website or contact them for information on upcoming events and any modifications to the farm's usual working hours.

- **The Met Cloisters**

The Met Cloisters, a unique division of The Metropolitan Museum of Art devoted to medieval European art and architecture, is perched at **99 Margaret Corbin Dr., New York, NY 10040** on a hill with a view of the Hudson River. Founded in 1938, this one-of-a-kind museum transports guests to the medieval era with its breathtaking building, verdant grounds, and vast art collection. The extraordinary architecture of the Met Cloisters that combines aspects of four ancient French monasteries, is much praised. Because of the museum's architectural style that emulates the calm, seclusion of medieval monastic life, visitors are given the impression that they are traveling back in time. The museum's layout includes a number of courtyards, garden areas, and a grand central courtyard with a peaceful haven from the bustling metropolis below.

The Met Cloisters becomes a wintry paradise for Christmas. The tranquility of the season and the occasional dusting of snow give the museum's medieval gardens, albeit inactive throughout the winter, a calm beauty. For a distinctive Christmas experience, The Cloisters is the perfect place to go because of its festive decorations that perfectly match its historical beauty. The celebrations of the season are set against a magnificent background of medieval artwork and architectural features found in the museum, like its stone carvings and Gothic arches. Winter strolls around the gardens are enjoyable, as the stillness and fresh air make for a tranquil respite from the hectic holiday season. Some of the best specimens of medieval art can be seen in the museum's exhibitions, like the well-known Unicorn Tapestries that seem especially striking against the winter sky. The collection's jewel are these tapestries, featuring fantastical unicorns in intricate settings and providing a mystical touch to the winter visit.

Perfect for a weekend getaway, The Met Cloisters is open every day from 10 a.m. to 5 p.m. and closed on Wednesdays. The inside of the museum is just as wonderful as the outside. Highlights include the galleries and chapels that showcase a variety of religious and secular medieval artworks, as well as the Treasury, having an amazing collection of medieval treasures and antiques. Notable are the gardens in the Cloisters, with flora and design that echoes medieval gardening techniques. The gardens nonetheless offer a tranquil setting for reflection and relaxation, even if they lack color in the winter. The gardens are available for exploration and burst with color throughout the warmer months, adding to the museum's allure. The

Met Cloisters charges $17 per person for admission; residents of New York, New Jersey, and Connecticut are admitted free of charge. This makes it a location that both residents and visitors can easily reach. The well-maintained museum has many features, such as a gift store selling a variety of souvenirs and products with medieval themes, a small café, and bathrooms.

FESTIVE SHOPPING EXPERIENCES

Budget Friendly Shopping Destinations

Holiday markets are a wonderful place to browse for unique and affordable gifts while enjoying the festive atmosphere. There are a ton of alternatives available at these markets for everyone on your list, often including local food vendors, artisans, and artists:

- **Chelsea Market**

 The premier indoor marketplace Chelsea Market, located at **75 9th Ave., New York, NY 10011**, is well-known for its eclectic blend of dining, shopping, and unique experiences. This spot, open daily from 7 AM to 10 PM, is well-known for its wide selection of offers and upbeat atmosphere, particularly around the holidays. Chelsea Market is a gourmet paradise for foodies.

There is an abundance of delectable cuisine available to satisfy any palate. The Lobster Place delivers fresh scallops and delectable lobster rolls, among other fresh seafood entrees. Sarabeth's Bakery offers a delectable selection of sweet pastries and baked goods. With its unique spices, gourmet cheeses, handcrafted bread, and other specialty items, the market is a favored spot for both everyday shopping and special occasions. Chelsea Market has an extensive assortment of small stores in addition to eateries. At artisans & Fleas, one-of-a-kind finds an eclectic assortment of vintage items, handcrafted jewelry, and distinctive home décor from local artisans.

The design of the market blends industrial flair with historic charm. The combination of an exposed brick wall, high ceilings, and an open floor plan makes for a warm and inviting atmosphere. Christmastime at Chelsea Market is especially beautiful. The space is filled with festive lights and decorations that heighten the atmosphere and sets a beautiful backdrop for an unforgettable stay. Chelsea Market is a crowded place because it hosts many events so there are always new experiences.

Visitors can explore both the market and the lovely park by The High Line, an elevated park that runs alongside the market for another dimension of interest.

- **The Shops at Columbus Circle**

 The Columbus Circle Holiday Market, located at **Columbus Cir & Central Park S, New York, NY 10019,** offers a traditional New York City holiday atmosphere. This charming market is a joyous occasion during the holidays when local business owners and artists showcase their creations, artwork, home accessories, and a wide selection of delectable snacks.

The Columbus Circle Holiday Market offers an incredible selection of unique gifts and handcrafted items. The market has a broad variety of stalls offering handcrafted jewelry, fashionable apparel, eco-friendly products, and gorgeous home décor. Visit each station to find distinctive products that capture the essence of the season. Often local artisans, the merchants offer the things on exhibit a personal touch. Similar delectable dining options can be found at Columbus Circle, including a wide selection of international cuisines and gourmet sweets. Well-liked vendors include German Delights, renowned for its classic gingerbread and Christmas gifts, and Wonderen Stroopwafels from the Netherlands, providing warm, fresh stroopwafels in addition to ready-to-go options. The market's food court serves delectable meals and snacks, although prices may be a touch higher there. You'll pay a premium for cheese wheel pasta, handcrafted desserts, and gourmet hot tea.

The market is surrounded with festive décor, like flowers and twinkling lights that gives it a warm and welcoming atmosphere. The charming setup, complete with cozy booths and glittering lights, adds to the holiday spirit and creates a stunning backdrop for Christmas shopping. The Columbus Circle Holiday Market is a terrific spot to stop before or after seeing Central Park. It's located at the base of the Time Warner Center, right next to the park.

- **Bank of America Winter Village at Bryant Park**

The most popular winter attraction in New York is the Bank of America Winter Village, located in Bryant Park at 41st **Street and 6th Avenue, New York, NY 10018.** October 27 to early January is when the park is turned into a fantastical vacation destination. With a range of activities and sights that appropriately represent the mood of the season, this joyful oasis is a must-see.

Situated in the heart of Winter Village, this 17,000-square-foot ice skating rink is renowned for its picturesque surroundings. The rink is a lovely place, with the city skyline and Christmas lights reflecting off the ice, creating a wonderful scene.. To guarantee a place, tickets should be reserved in advance. This popular attraction is suitable for skaters of all ability levels, and rentals are available for those without their gear. Keep in mind that all personal belongings, including bags and phones, must be placed in designated areas before hitting the ice. Adjacent to the rink is The Lodge, a welcoming bar and dining area with an extensive menu. This is a wonderful place for a casual supper with a festive touch or a warm-up after skating. BThe Christmas shops are arranged by Urbanspace Markets around the rink and include a charming assortment of stalls for visitors to peruse. These stores sell a variety of products, including gourmet meals, ornaments for the holidays, unique crafts, and handcrafted gifts. The market is a veritable treasure trove of items for Christmas shopping, catering to a broad spectrum of preferences and budgets.

You can reserve one of the comfortable igloos in Winter Village for a more intimate experience. These cozy, heated spaces offer a welcome respite from the bustling market and are perfect for dining, mingling, or lounging in a unique, small-group setting. Keep in mind reservations are required, and renting an igloo is a leisurely way to prolong your visit. Another attraction in Winter Village is the Curling Cafe & Bar, where you can play the traditional curling game. This intriguing game is a wonderful way to spend time with friends and family and adds a unique touch to your winter vacation. Energy-boosting snacks and beverages are available in the café throughout your curling session.

SAMPLE FESTIVE ITINERARIES

A 7-Day Christmas Itinerary for Families with Kids

Day 1

- To start your family vacation, visit the Christmas Tree at Rockefeller Center. Take in this famous show, and then go ice skating at The Rink at Rockefeller Center for an incredible experience.

- Take a stroll through Bryant Park's Winter Village. The kids will enjoy looking at the booths and taking in the holiday spirit. You might want to go ice skating again at Bryant Park's rink before getting warm with hot chocolate.

- To end the day, visit Macy's Winter Décor on 34th Street. It's a holiday wonderland full of lights and magical window displays.

Day 2

- Go up to the New York Botanical Garden. Kids love it because the little trains zoom through models of famous New York City sites.

- In the afternoon, catch the spectacular Radio City Christmas Spectacular with the Rockettes. You and your family will be amazed by the beautiful outfits and performances.

- Enjoy a family-friendly dinner near Times Square, surrounded by the dazzling city lights.

Day 3

- Dive into the city's rich history by visiting the New York Historical Society, offering child-friendly exhibits alongside festive displays.
- Next, make your way to the Museum at Eldridge Street, a beautifully renovated

synagogue that adds cultural depth to your holiday experience.

- For a change of pace, visit the nearby Tenement Museum to see how immigrant families enjoyed the holidays in historical New York.

- Wrap up the day with a stop at St. Patrick's Cathedral, where the stunning Gothic building is lit by holiday lights.

Day 4

- Take a trip to Brooklyn to explore the famous Dyker Heights Christmas Lights. This neighborhood goes all out with larger-than-life decorations and sparkling lights that will mesmerize the kids.

- Before going back to Manhattan, visit the Brooklyn Heights Promenade for amazing views of the city skyline, or catch the sunset from the Edge or Top of the Rock.

- If time allows, visit Brooklyn's Greenwood Cemetery for a quiet, reflective walk through its winter scenery.

Day 5

- Start your morning with a delicious Christmas brunch at Clinton St. Baking Company or the cozy Russ & Daughters Cafe.

- After brunch, explore NYC's lesser-known holiday gems like the Morris-Jumel Mansion or the Merchant's House Museum, both beautifully dressed for the season.

- Head to Washington Square Park to enjoy more holiday lights and perhaps a family shot beneath the arch, followed by a visit to The Met Cloisters for a quiet, scenic escape.

- For unique gifts and treats, wrap up shopping at Chelsea Market or Winter Village at Bryant Park.

Day 6

- On Christmas Eve, visit one of the stunning churches, like St. Francis of Assisi Roman Catholic Church or Basilica of St. Patrick's Old Cathedral, for a holiday service that will fill your family with the warmth of the season.

- In the evening, watch a holiday performance at The Players Theatre or Theater for the New City, where family-friendly shows with a festive twist are sure to please.

- If you're feeling brave, take in some of the city's festive lights by visiting places like Miracle on 9th Street or Gallow Green for a holiday-themed treat or drink (parents only!).

Day 7

- Start Christmas morning with brunch at Good Enough to Eat or Friedman's, offering classic comfort foods that the whole family will love.

- After brunch, spend a peaceful Christmas Day visiting the Queens County Farm Museum for a rustic holiday experience or explore Bronx Little Italy for a festive walk and holiday shopping.

- End your holiday adventure with a ride to One World Observatory for a breathtaking 360-degree view of New York City aglow with Christmas lights. It's a magical way to end your family's holiday adventure in the Big Apple.

A 7-day Christmas itinerary for couples

Day 1

- Start your romantic holiday by visiting the famous Rockefeller Center's Christmas Tree. Take some shots together under the twinkling lights before going to The Rink at Rockefeller Center for a dreamy ice-skating session.

- Take a cozy stroll over to Bryant Park Winter Village, where the holiday market offers charming stalls filled with unique gifts and festive treats. End the day with hot cocoa or mulled wine as you visit the park.

- If you're up for more skating, enjoy a twilight skate at Wollman Rink in Central Park, surrounded by the city skyline and holiday lights.

Day 2

- Start your day with a walk through Union Square Holiday Market, picking up handmade gifts or warming up with some festive street food.

- At noon, enjoy the magic of the Radio City Christmas Spectacular with the Rockettes. The joyful environment and awe-inspiring acts make for a perfect date.

- As evening falls, take in the beautiful views of the city from Top of the Rock or Edge.

- Watch the sun set behind the Manhattan skyline and enjoy a sweeping view of the city's holiday lights from above.

Day 3

- Dive onto New York's rich history with a visit to the New York Historical Society, where you'll find holiday exhibits alongside fascinating historical displays.

- Afterward, explore the beautifully renovated Museum at Eldridge Street, where the stunning building sets a quiet holiday mood.

- For a deeper dive into the city's past, head to the Tenement Museum to learn how immigrant families enjoyed the holidays in a bygone age.

- End your day with a quiet, reflective visit to Trinity Church, taking in the beauty of its holiday decorations and peaceful atmosphere.

Day 4

- Spend the day exploring Brooklyn, starting with the amazing Dyker Heights Christmas Lights. Wander hand in hand through the streets as you enjoy the over-the-top holiday decorations, a true winter beauty.

- For a quieter moment, visit the Brooklyn Heights Promenade for sweeping views of

Manhattan's skyline offer a romantic setting.

- If time permits, stop by the Morris-Jumel Mansion or Brooklyn's Greenwood Cemetery to enjoy a more personal, beautiful experience away from the hustle and bustle of the city.

- Return to Manhattan for a cozy dinner and a festive drink at Oscar Wilde or Gallow Green, both decked out for the holidays.

Day 5

- Begin your day with a leisurely brunch at Russ & Daughters Cafe or Clinton St. Baking Company, both offering cozy, personal settings perfect for a romantic holiday morning.

- Spend the afternoon exploring the Bank of America Winter Village at Bryant Park or The Shops at Columbus Circle for last-minute gifts or special holiday finds.

- If you're up for some adventure, head to Washington Square Park to see its festive arch and lights, then take a short trip to The Met Cloisters for a calm, medieval-themed holiday escape.

Day 6

- On Christmas Eve, attend a candlelight service at the Cathedral Church of St. John the Divine or Church of St. Ignatius Loyola. The serious beauty of the services will strengthen the holiday spirit.

- In the evening, treat yourselves to a special dinner at one of the city's holiday-themed spots, like Miracle on 9th Street, where festive drinks and cozy atmospheres make for the perfect holiday date night.

- After dinner, take a romantic walk along the city's lively streets, taking in the bright lights and magical holiday ambiance.

Day 7

- Start Christmas morning with a beautiful brunch at Good Enough to Eat or Jack's Wife Freda, where the cozy, laid-back setting is ideal for a special Christmas morning meal.

- Spend the rest of the day visiting One World Observatory for amazing views of the city bathed in Christmas lights. This will be the perfect time to reflect on the beautiful week you've spent together.

- For a more personal, low-key experience, you could visit Bronx Little Italy or the Queens County Farm Museum to enjoy a slower-paced Christmas afternoon away from the city crowds.

SAFETY ADVICE AND PRACTICAL TIPS

Staying Safe During the Holidays

Finding a balance between the thrill of the season and cautious safety precautions is essential to staying safe. With twinkling lights, festive markets, and well-known events like the Rockefeller Center tree lighting, the city becomes a wintry wonderland. To make your vacation safe and enjoyable, you must be vigilant and make thoughtful decisions among the chaos.

- Above all, be aware of your surroundings, particularly in crowded areas like Times Square, Fifth Avenue, or Christmas markets. Pickpocketing might be an issue in large crowds, so it's a sensible idea to secure your belongings. Carry your purse or backpack in front of you rather than on your back.

- To take advantage of the vibrant nightlife of the city, remain on well-known, well-lit avenues and steer clear of isolated locations after dark.

- planning your transportation is a good idea, whether that means taking use of the extensive rail system, using a ride-sharing service, or renting a familiar yellow automobile.

- Keep in mind that during holidays, the metro can become packed. Keep an eye on your possessions, and avoid sleeping in unoccupied train cars after dark.

- Wintertime in the city offers additional challenges of its own. Take your time and wear sturdy, non-slip shoes, as walking on ice and slushy roadways can be hazardous.

- If you're traveling during the holidays, give yourself extra time to go around because there will be a lot of traffic and slick roads.

- Pedestrians should always abide by all traffic signs and use the designated crosswalks. Following the weather forecast is also a good idea because unexpected snowstorms can throw preparations into a loop.

Having emergency contacts and a portable phone charger handy is usually a smart idea, more so if you anticipate spending a lot of time on the road.

Money and Currency

Most establishments in New York accept mobile payments. The US dollar (USD) serves as the foundation for the city. To make things easier and more affordable, know when to utilize each kind of payment.

- Having cash on hand is a good idea, particularly for smaller purchases or when visiting establishments such as local markets, elderly homes, or street vendors that may not accept debit or credit cards.

- Credit and debit cards are widely accepted in the city and are used for the bulk of transactions at stores, transportation companies, and other establishments.

- Having cash on hand will also help you avoid issues since certain businesses, particularly smaller ones, could impose a minimum purchase amount when accepting credit or debit cards.

- While making a cash payment, keep in mind that tipping is customary in many service contexts. Tipping normally consists of 15% to 20% of the total bill at restaurants, a few dollars per drink at bars, and additional gratuities for taxi drivers and hotel employees.

- It is something foreign visitors should consider to exchange currencies. Airports and designated currency exchange kiosks allow you to convert currencies, but sometimes these places give better exchange rates.

- With a debit card, it's simpler to withdraw cash directly from an ATM because they frequently have better conversion rates. And, you should ask your bank about any possible overseas fees.

- In terms of expenses, it's also important to inform your bank of your travel schedule to avoid any issues arising from reporting your card for irregular usage. Mobile payment options like Apple Pay, Google Wallet, and others are a smart option, as they are often accepted if you would like not to accept cash or credit cards.

To ensure that you're touring the city that never sleeps without running into any financial difficulties, the best method is to always be prepared with a range of payment options at your disposal.

Emergency Contacts and Information

When visiting, it's important to be prepared for any situation, and that includes knowing how to reach emergency contacts and information.

- The international emergency number in the United States, including New York City, is 911. This number should be your first call in any life-threatening emergency or if you require instant help from police, fire services, or medical crises. It's important to know that 911 workers in New York are trained to handle international calls, so if English is not your first language, you can still get the help you need. Provide clear and straightforward information about your position and the nature of the situation to ensure that help comes as quickly as possible.

- For non-emergency situations, like reporting noise problems, graffiti, or other local issues, New York City has a specific line: 311.

This number is useful for getting information on city services, sharing non-urgent concerns, or asking general questions about New York's public services. It can be reached via phone, email, or web, and it's open 24/7.

- If you or someone in your party has been introduced to a harmful substance, the New York City Poison Control Center can be reached at (212) 764-7667 or (800) 222-1222. They provide quick help and assistance 24/7.

- In the event of an emergency on the subway, you can use the intercoms placed on platforms and in train cars to call the train driver or station staff. It's also a beneficial idea to familiarize yourself with train exits and emergency measures marked in stops. For general transportation problems, the MTA (Metropolitan Transportation Authority) can be reached at (718) 330-1234.

- If you lose an item on the train, bus, or other public transportation, call the MTA Lost and Found Office at (646) 252-1701 or visit their office at 34th Street-Penn Station. For lost things in cabs, call 311 and provide the taxi's plate number, date, and time of the ride.

For foreign tourists, having the contact information for your country's office in New York City is important. Consulates can provide assistance in situations like lost documents, legal problems, or if you find yourself in need of help while abroad. The U.S. Department of State's website shows all foreign consulates in New York. Here are a few of the important ones:

- British Consulate General: Located at 845 Third Avenue, New York, NY 10022. They can be reached at (212) 745-0200.

- Consulate General of Canada: Located at 466 Lexington Avenue, 20th Floor, New York, NY 10017. Their contact number is (844) 880-6519.

- Consulate General of Australia: Located at 150 East 42nd Street, New York, NY 10017. They can be reached at (212) 351-6500.

New York City can experience a range of weather conditions, like snowstorms in the winter. It's important to stay updated about any adverse weather that might affect your plans. The National Weather Service (NWS) offers up-to-date information on weather conditions, and you can sign up for updates through Notify NYC, the city's official emergency communications program. This service will send you alerts via text, email, or phone about severe weather, travel delays, and other situations.

- In the rare event of a natural disaster, New York City has designated emergency shelters throughout the five boroughs. These centers are triggered during large-scale situations and can provide safety, food, and medical assistance. Information about shelter sites can be received through 311 or the city's disaster management website.

New York has made major steps to ensure mobility for people with disabilities. For those who cannot use public transportation due to a disability. In an emergency, it's important to know your exact escape plan and have an emergency contact who is aware of your position and needs.

- The Mayor's Office for People with Disabilities (MOPD) gives extra tools and can be reached at (212) 788-2830.

Staying informed, prepared, and knowing how to access the right tools will help you feel more safe and confident as you explore all that New York City has to offer and these sources and information will ensure that you have the help you need to handle any situation that happens.

MERRY CHRISTMAS

Your New York holiday is sure to be unforgettable, as the city's glittering lights dance over the skyline and the holiday spirit permeates every area. New York sets up a remarkable Christmas experience that mixes tradition, excitement, and a sense of awe. For your vacation, this guide has described some of the must do locations, activities, and hidden treasures to experience. It's your job now to create the ideal Christmas plan that reflects your preferences and hobbies.

And whatever your preferences, these places come with a great starting point for organizing your celebration. You can follow the sample itineraries exactly or feel free to add and subtract from it as you see fit. Remember to allow time for the spontaneous walks through snow-dusted streets, a warm cup of cocoa from a neighborhood café, or the joyful carolers spreading happiness in Central Park; these are the moments that really make the holidays unique. As you learn, remember that New York is about the experience as well as the place.

Allow yourself to get carried away by the energy of the city, embrace the spirit of the occasion, and create memories that will last long after the Christmas décor has been taken down. Cheers to a Christmas full of happiness, fun, and New York City's distinct beauty.

Made in the USA
Columbia, SC
26 November 2024

47614350R00107